P9-CTP-372

THE WAY OF MEN

"Jack Donovan has written a thought-provoking treatise on the essential struggle of men, taking on timeless concepts, in an honest examination of what manhood means to him. The book is carefully reasoned with his own impressive, self-made intellect. He's done his research, and pondered deep, and while I didn't always agree with everything he said—I am a better man for reading it."

—Sam Sheridan, author of *A Fighter's Heart*

"Generation Zero is the generation of Sesame Street and Ritalin, a generation raised without any memory or first-hand knowledge of a world in which masculinity was encouraged and celebrated rather than punished. *The Way of Men* is the first complete roadmap to masculinity ever published, the truth your fathers never told you. For the men of my generation, this book is beyond invaluable."

—Ferdinand Bardamu, *InMalaFide*.com

"A thought-provoking read on what it means to be a man today in a world that's increasingly finding masculinity undesirable and un-needed. Donovan makes bold and unapologetic arguments on what The Way of Men needs to be in the future."

—Brett McKay, author of *The Art of Manliness, Manvotionals*

"In an age where traditional masculinity is disparaged, deconstructed, feared and scorned, Jack Donovan has engaged in the necessary task of reconstructing what masculinity is, and how it fits into modern society. It seems unlikely that one could learn manhood from a book, but this would be a good place to try."

—Scott Locklin; writer, *Taki's Magazine*

Jack Donovan's latest book, *The Way of Men*, cuts through the Marxist and politically correct platitudes suffocating mainstream sociology and anthropology to deliver an insightful, original, and data-driven analysis of tribalism, gender relations, and the tortured state of manliness in the post-modern age.

—Matt Parrott, Blogger and Author of *Hoosier Nation*

"While others in the "Man-centric" blogosphere prefer to critique crazy feminists or theorize about the best way to pick up unstable women at bars, Jack Donovan has taken up the more important, anthropological task of asking who "the Man" really is."

—Richard Spencer, Editor of *Alternative Right*

"*The Way of Men* reads like a primer for a generation that didn't know it needed one. Donovan's athletic prose reads quickly, and cuts straight to the point: Only in a coddled nanny-state could entire generations of boys grow up never having to put themselves to the hazards that harden boys into men."

—Max. US Army, Infantry

THE WAY OF MEN

JACK DONOVAN

DISSONANT HUM

2012

First electronic edition released March 26, 2012.
ASIN: B007O0Y1ZE

First paperback edition.
ISBN-10: 0985452307
ISBN-13: 978-0-9854523-0-8

Cover Design and Artwork by Jack Donovan.

Published by Jack Donovan

[DH]

[DISSONANT HUM]
4230 SE King Road, No. 185
Milwaukie, Oregon, 97222
USA.

www.dissonant-hum.com

Subjects:

1. Social Sciences - Men's Studies
2. Masculinity
3. Psychology - Men
4. Men - Social Conditions
5. Masculinity - History
6. Evolutionary Psychology
7. Sex role
8. Gender Studies
9. Philosophy

CONTENTS

...gangsta culture is the essence of patriarchal masculinity.

—bell hooks

PREFACE

I present this book to you without ego.

It is not an advertisement for my own manhood or a boast to flatter the men of my own tribe.

This book is my answer to the question: "What is masculinity?"

If men are a certain way, and there is a way to be manly, then: "What is The Way of Men?"

For decades, people have been talking about a "crisis" of masculinity. Our leaders have created a world in spite of men, a world that refuses to accept who men are and doesn't care what they want. Our world asks men to change "for the better," but offers men less of value to them than their fathers and grandfathers had. The voices who speak for the future say that men must abandon their old way and find a new way. But what is that way and where does it lead?

As I came to understand The Way of Men, I became more concerned about where men are today, and where they are headed. I wondered if there was a way for men to follow their own way into a future that belongs to men.

That's the path of this book. My answers may not be the kind of answers you want to hear, but they are the only answers that satisfied my inquiry.

Jack Donovan
March 2012
Milwaukie, Oregon

THE WAY OF MEN IS THE WAY OF THE GANG

When someone tells a man to be a man, they mean that there is a *way* to be a man. A man is not just a thing to be—it is also a way to be, a path to follow and a way to walk. Some try to make manhood mean everything. Others believe that it means nothing at all. Being good at being a man can't mean everything, but it has always meant something.

Most traditions have viewed masculinity and femininity as complementary opposites. It makes sense to say that masculinity is that which is least feminine and femininity is that which is least masculine, but saying that doesn't tell us much about The Way of Men.

Boys and girls don't pair off at birth and scurry off to a dank cave together. Humans have always been social animals. We live in cooperative groups. Our bodies sort us into groups of males or females. We interact socially as members of one group or the other. These groups aren't arbitrary or cultural—they're basic and biological. Males have to negotiate male and female groups as males. Males aren't simply reacting to females. We react to other males, as males. Who we are has a lot to do with how we see ourselves in relationship to other males, as members of the male group.

A man is not merely a man but a man among men, in a world of men. Being good at being a man has more to do with a man's ability to succeed with men and within groups of men than it does with a man's relationship to any woman or any group of women. When someone tells a man to be a man, they are telling him to be more like other men, more like the majority of men, and ideally more like the men whom other men hold in high regard.

Women believe they can improve men by making masculinity about what women want from men. Men want women to want them, but female approval isn't the only thing men care about. When men compete against each other for status, they are competing for *each other's* approval. The women whom men find most desirable have historically been attracted to—or been claimed by—men who were feared or revered by other men. Female approval has regularly been a consequence of male approval.

Masculinity is about being a man within a group of men. Above all things, **masculinity is about what men want from each other**.

If The Way of Men seems confusing, it is only because there are so many different groups of men who want so many different things from men. Established men of wealth and power have always wanted men to believe that being a man was about duty and obedience, or that manhood could be proved by attaining wealth and power through established channels. Men of religion and ideology have always wanted men to believe that being a man was a spiritual or moral endeavor, and that manhood could be proved through various means of self-mastery, self-denial, self-sacrifice or evangelism. Men who have something to sell have always wanted men to believe that masculinity can be proved or improved by buying it.

In a united tribe with a strong sense of its own identity, there is some harmony between the interests of male groups, and The Way of Men seems straightforward enough. In a complex, cosmopolitan, individualistic, disunited civilization with many thin, à la carte identities, The Way of Men is unclear. The ways touted by rich and powerful men are tossed with the ways of gurus and ideologues and jumbled with the macho trinkets of merchants in such a mess that it's easy to see why some say masculinity can mean anything, everything, or nothing at all. Add to that the "improvements" suggested by women and The Way of Men becomes an unreadable map to a junkyard of ideals.

To understand who men are, what they have in common and why men struggle to prove their worth to each other, reduce male groups to their nucleic form. Sprawling, complex civilizations made up of millions of people are relatively new to men. For most of their time on this planet, men have organized in small survival bands, set against a hostile environment, competing for women and resources with other bands of men. Understanding the way men react to each other demands an understanding of their most basic social unit. Understanding what men want from each other requires an understanding of what men have most often needed from each other, and a sense of how these needs have shaped masculine psychology.

Relieved of moral pretense and stripped of folk costumes, the raw masculinity that all men know in their gut has to do with being good at being a man within a small, embattled gang of men struggling to survive.

The Way of Men is the way of that gang.

THE PERIMETER

You are part of a small human group fighting to stay alive.

The reason why doesn't matter.

Conquest, war, death, hunger or disease—any of The Horsemen will do.

You could be our primal ancestors, you could be pioneers, you could be stranded in some remote location, you could be survivors of a nuclear holocaust or the zombie apocalypse. Again, it doesn't matter. For humans without access to advanced technology, the scenario plays out more or less the same way.

You have to define your group. You need to define who is in and who is out, and you need to identify potential threats. You need to create and maintain some sort of safe zone around the perimeter of your group. Everyone will have to contribute to the group's survival in some way unless the group agrees to protect and feed someone who can't contribute due to age or illness. For those who can work, you'll need to decide who does what, based on what they are good at, who works well together, and what makes the most practical sense.

HUNTING AND FIGHTING

Hunting and fighting are two of the most dangerous jobs you'll need to do to stay alive.

To thrive, humans need protein and fat. You can get enough protein and fat from vegetables, but without an established farm you're going to be hard pressed to gather enough vegetables to meet your nutritional needs. A large animal can provide protein and fat for days—longer if you know how to preserve the meat.

The problem with big, protein-rich animals is that they don't want to die. Meat is muscle, and muscle makes animals strong—often stronger than men. Wild beasts come equipped with tusks, antlers, hooves, claws and sharp teeth. They're going to fight for their lives. Taking down a big, protein-rich animal is going to be dangerous. It will require strength, courage, technique, and teamwork. Finding food also requires exploring—venturing out into the unknown—and who knows what lurks *out there*?

If you are going to survive, your group will need protection from predators—animal, human, alien, or undead. If there is someone or something *out there* who wants what you have and is willing to fight for it, you're going to need to figure out who in your group is going to be willing to fight back. You'll want the people who are best at fighting to stand watch, to defend everything you care about, or to go out and eliminate a potential threat. If someone or something has something that you need, the best way to get it may be to take it. *Who in your group will be willing and able to do that?*

Maybe females are part of your group. Maybe they aren't. If females are with you, they won't have access to reliable birth control. Males and females won't stop having sex, and females will get pregnant. Humans are mammals, and like most mammals, a greater part of the reproductive burden will fall on women. That's not fair, but *nature isn't fair.* Even strong, aggressive women become more vulnerable and less mobile during pregnancy. Even tough women will nurse their young. They'll bond with their offspring and take to caring for them quickly. Babies are helpless, and children are vulnerable for years.

If there were no other physical or mental differences between women and men, in a hostile environment the biological realities of human reproduction would still mean that over time more men would be charged with exploring, hunting, fighting, building, and defending. Men would have more time to specialize and develop the necessary skills to excel at those tasks. They wouldn't have a good excuse not to.

Men will never get pregnant, they will never be nursing, and they will be less encumbered by their children. They may not even know who their children are. *Women know who their kids are.* Children don't depend on their fathers in the same way that they depend on their mothers. Men are freer to take risks for the good of the group, believing that their offspring will live on.

As things are, there are biological differences between men and women that have little to do with pregnancy or breastfeeding. On average, men are bigger and stronger than women. Men are more daring, probably more mechanically inclined, and generally better at navigating. Men are hard wired for aggressive play. High testosterone men take more risks and seek more thrills. Men are more interested in competing for status, and when they win, their bodies give them a dopamine high and *more testosterone.* [1]

Because your group is struggling to survive, every choice matters. If you give the wrong person the wrong job, that person could die, you could die, another person could die, or you could all die. Because of the differences between the sexes, the best person for jobs that involve exploring, hunting, fighting, building, or defending is usually going to be a male. This is not some arbitrary cultural prejudice; it is the kind of vital strategic discrimination that will keep your group alive.

Humans, like chimpanzees, will often hunt in teams because cooperative hunting is more effective than hunting alone. When you put together a team—any kind of team— the raw skills of your candidates aren't the only factors you have to consider. You also have to consider the team's social dynamic. Which people will work best together? As a leader, you want to create synergy, reduce distractions, and avoid conflicts within the group. Males will compete for status within any group, but they will also compete for females. Eliminating a second layer of potential jealousy and antagonism may be reason enough to choose a male over a female.

---

1   Some studies have shown a major decrease in male testosterone over the last 20 years (see below). That drop may be due to something in the water but it's likely a result of widespread obesity. I'd bet it also has something to with a relative loss of social status and the proliferation of safe, sedentary lifestyles. If testosterone really has dropped in a few decades, it proves that men and women were *more* different in the past and that future studies claiming similarities between the sexes will be less relevant when looking at historical ideas about sex differences.

Travison, Thomas G., Andre B. Araujo, Amy B. O'Donnell, Varant Kupelian, and John B. McKinlay. "A Population-Level Decline in Serum Testosterone Levels in American Men." *The Journal of Clinical Endocrinology & Metabolism* 92.11 Jan. (2007): 196-202. Web. 5 Dec. 2011.

If there are females in your group, they will have plenty of hard and necessary work to do. Everyone will have to pull their own weight, but the hunting and fighting is almost always going to be up to the men. When lives are on the line, people will drop the etiquette of equality and make that decision again and again because it makes the most sense.

That practical division of labor is where the male world begins.

THE PARTY-GANG   *Warre*

Thomas Hobbes wrote that when men live without fear of a common power, they live in a state of "*warre*." In *warre*, every man is against every other man.

Hobbes' idea of *warre* is interesting on a theoretical level, but his *warre* of all against all is not the state of nature for men. It's natural for a man to look after his own interests, but those interests drive men together—*quickly*. A loner has no one to ask for help, no one to watch his back, no one to guard him when he sleeps. Men have a greater chance of survival together than they do apart. Men have always hunted and fought in small teams. The natural state of *warre* is ongoing conflict between small gangs of men.

Chimpanzees organize on a party-gang basis, which means they change the size of their groups depending on the circumstances. Chimps gather together in large parties and build alliances for strategic reasons, for mating, and for the sharing of resources. When circumstances change, they break into smaller groups and hunting parties. The smaller groups—the gangs—are the tightest and most stable. The males are loyal and rarely move from gang to gang. Females sometimes join the males in hunting activities, but they are more likely to move from one gang to another over time.

Men organize the same way.

For example, take military units.

>Army: 80,000 – 200,000 members
>
>Corps: 20,000 – 45,000 members
>
>Division: 10,000 – 15,000 members
>
>Brigade: 3,000 – 5,000 members
>
>Regiment: 3,000 – 5,000 members
>
>Battalion: 300 – 1,300 members
>
>Company: 80 – 225 members
>
>Platoon: 26 – 55 members
>
>Section/Patrol/Squad: 8 – 13 members
>
>Fireteam: 2 – 4 members

All of the men in a given army are part of the same big team, but the strength of the bonds between men will increase as the size of the unit decreases. In smaller groups, men are more loyal to one another.

When writer Sebastian Junger asked US soldiers in Afghanistan about their allegiances, they told him that, "they would unhesitatingly risk their lives for anyone in the platoon or company, but that sentiment dropped off pretty quickly after that. By the time you got to brigade level—three or four thousand men—any sense of common goals or identity was pretty much theoretical."[2] There is frequently rivalry between the groups. Each group has its own regalia, its own traditions, its own symbolism, and a common history.

---

2   Junger, Sebastian. *WAR*. Hachette Book Group, 2010. 242. Print.

Some researchers believe that the human brain can only process enough information to maintain meaningful relationships with 150 or so people at any given time.[3] That's about the size of a military company, but also about the size of a typical primitive human tribe, and roughly the number of "friends" most people contact regularly through social networking sites.

Within that tribe of 150, people form even smaller groups. How many people would you loan a lot of money to? How many people could you depend on in an emergency? How many people could depend on you?

If you're like most, that number drops to the size of a platoon, a squad, or even a fireteam. The team size for most group sports is somewhere between the fireteam number and the platoon number. American football teams have around 50 members on a roster, but only 11 are on the field at one time. Baseball teams keep 25 members on their rosters, with 9 on the field. Soccer teams play between 7 and 11 members. Basketball teams play 5. Water polo teams put 7 in the pool.

Men revert back to this archetypal gang size, even for recreation and storytelling. How many main characters are there in your favorite films, books, or television shows? The number works for religion and myth, too. Jesus had 12 apostles. How many Greek gods can you name? Norse?

The group of 2 to 15 men is a comfort zone. It's an effective team size for tactical maneuvers, but it's also socially manageable. You can *really know* about that many guys at one

3   W. -X. Zhou, D. Sornette, R. A. Hill and R. I. M. Dunbar. "Discrete Hierarchical Organization of Social Group Sizes" *Proceedings: Biological Sciences* , Vol. 272, No. 1561 (Feb. 22, 2005), pp. 439-444.

Also: Search "Dunbar's Number" or review articles about scientist Robin Dunbar.

time. You can maintain a good working relationship and a meaningful social history with 100 or so more. Beyond those numbers, connections become extremely superficial, trust breaks down, and more rules and codes—always enforced by the threat of violence—are required to keep men "together." In times of stress—when resources are scarce, when the system of rules and codes breaks down, when there is a lapse in enforcement, or when men have little to lose and more to gain by breaking the law—it is The Way of Men to break off from large parties and operate in small, nimble gangs.

The fireteam-to-platoon sized gang is the smallest unit of *us*. Beyond *us* is *them*, and the line that separates *us* from *them* is a circle of trust.

DRAWING THE PERIMETER

The first job of men in dire times has always been to establish and secure "the perimeter."

Imagine yourself again in our survival scenario. People can't fight and hunt and kill all day and all night forever. Humans have to sleep, they have to eat, and they need downtime. You need to create a safe space and set up camp somewhere.

You'll also have to identify some desirable resources, like access to water and food. One of the first things you have to consider is whether the spot makes you vulnerable to attack from predators or unknown groups of men. Then you do some basic recon—you check out the surrounding area to see if there is evidence of another tribe, or undesirable beasts. Tired and satisfied, you and your pals set up a base camp and keep an eye on a rudimentary perimeter.

The survival of your group will depend on your ability to successfully claim land and keep it safe.

When you claim territory and draw a perimeter, that line separates your group from the rest of the world. The people inside the perimeter become *us* and everything known and unknown outside the perimeter becomes *them*.

Beyond the light of your night fire, there is darkness. *They* lie just beyond the flicker of your fire, *out there* in the dark. *They* could be wild animals, zombies, killer robots, or dragons. *They* could also be other men. Men know what men need, and what they want. If your men have something that men want or need, you'll have to be wary of other men. The things that have value to men—tools, food, water, women, livestock, shelter or even good land—will have to be protected from other men who might be desperate enough to harm you to get those things. The perimeter separates men you trust from men you don't trust, or don't know well enough to trust.

People like to make friends. Being on the defensive all the time is stressful. Most people want to trust other people. Most people want to be able to relax. If you are smart, until you know *them*, *they* will remain *out there* on the other side of the perimeter. Even if you let your guard down to cooperate or trade with them, *they* may or may not be absorbed into *us*. As long as other men maintain separate identities, there is always the chance that *they* will choose to put the interests of *their own* ahead of your interests. In hard times, agreements between groups fall apart. Competition creates animosity, and men will dehumanize each other to make the tough decisions necessary for their own group to survive.

If you put males together for a short period of time and give them something to compete for, they will form a team of *us* vs. *them*. This was famously illustrated by Muzafer Sherif's "Robbers Cave Experiment." Social psychologists separated two groups of boys and forced them to compete. Each group of boys created a sense of *us* based on what they liked about themselves or how they wanted to imagine themselves. They also created negative caricatures of the other group. The groups became hostile toward each other. However, when the researchers gave them a good enough reason to cooperate, the competing gangs were able to put aside their differences and join together in a larger party.

It has always been the job of men to draw the perimeter, to establish a safe space, to separate *us* from *them* and create a circle of trust.

The discovery of new land in the Americas made it possible for men to do this again in recent human history. Small groups of men ventured out into unknown territory because they believed they had more to gain from risk than they could expect to gain through established channels in the old world. They braved the wild, set up camps, and reinvented civilization as the rest of the world looked on. Out there in the dark there were Injuns, bears, snakes, and other gangs of men willing to use violence to take whatever they wanted. Both the settlers and the natives were men under siege, and they had to harden themselves against external forces. They had to decide who they could trust, who they couldn't, and what they needed from the men around them.

The story of the American West is only one story. How many gangs, families, tribes and nations have been founded by a small group of men who struck out on their own, claimed land, defended it, made it safe and put down roots? If men had never done this, there would not be people living on every continent today.

A ROLE APART

You've decided who is in and who is out. You've decided who you trust, and who you don't. You are watching the perimeter, protecting what is inside the circle of flickering light, defending everything that means anything to you and the men who stand with you. It all comes down to you, the guardians, because you know that if you fail at your jobs there can be no human happiness, no family life, no storytelling, no art or music. Your role at the bloody edges of the boundary between *us* and *them* supersedes any role you have within the protected space. Yours is a role apart, and your value to the other men who share that responsibility will be determined by how well you are willing and able to fulfill that role.

Other men will need to know that they can depend on you, because everything matters, and your weakness, fear or incompetence could get any one of them killed or threaten the whole group. Men who are good at this job—men who are good at the job of being men—will earn the respect and trust of the group. Those men will be honored and treated better than men who are disloyal or undependable. The men who deliver victory at the moments of greatest peril will attain the highest status among men. They will be treated like heroes, and other men—especially young men—will emulate them.

In a complex society, almost all of us live deep within the perimeter. We create our own circles and cliques, and we defend them metaphorically. We include people or exclude them for all kinds of reasons. Far from any boundary between threat and safety, people celebrate qualities that have almost nothing to do with survival. The flock bleats for singers, designers, smooth talkers, and people whose only talents are being witty or pretty. The shepherds drive them round to more of the same.

When men evaluate each other *as men*, they still look for the same virtues that they'd need to keep the perimeter. Men respond to and admire the qualities that would make men useful and dependable in an emergency. Men have always had a role apart, and they still judge one another according to the demands of that role as a guardian in a gang struggling for survival against encroaching doom. Everything that is specifically about being a man—not merely a person—has to do with that role.

As you stand back to back, fending off incoming oblivion, what do you need from the men in your group? As you close a circle tighter around dangerous game that could feed you all for a week, what kind of men do you want at your flank?

THE TACTICAL VIRTUES

Vir is the Latin word for "man." The word "virtue" comes from the Latin *"virtus."* To the early Romans, *virtus* meant manliness, and manliness meant martial valor.[1] Demonstrating *virtus* meant showing strength and courage and loyalty to the tribe while attacking or defending against the enemies of Rome.

As the Romans became more successful and their civilization became more complex, it was no longer necessary for all men to hunt or fight. The fighting happened at the edge of the perimeter, and the fighting edge of Roman civilization moved outward. For men deep inside the circle, manliness became increasingly metaphorical.[2] Men who did other work could satisfy their need to be seen as men among men by fighting metaphorically, showing social courage, mastering their desires, and behaving ethically. The meaning of the word virtus and the Roman idea of manliness expanded to include values that were not merely survival virtues, but also civic and moral virtues.

---

1   McDonnell, Myles. *Roman Manliness : Virtus and the Roman Republic*. Cambridge University Press, 2006. 4. Print.

2   It is also true that manhood, by necessity, becomes increasingly metaphorical with age. An older man who can no longer compete with other men or hunt and fight will focus on developing other virtues.

Definitions of manliness expand to include other virtues as civilizations grow. However, these other virtues are less specific to men than the fighting virtues, and they vary more from culture to culture. "Civilized" virtue is about being a good person, a good citizen, a good member of a particular society. Manly virtues should be virtues directly related to manhood. The virtues that men all over the world recognize as manly virtues are the fighting virtues. Epics and action movies translate well because they appeal to something basic to the male condition—a desire to struggle and win, to fight for something, to fight for survival, to demonstrate your worthiness to other men.

The virtues associated specifically with being a man outline a rugged philosophy of living—a way to be that is also a strategy for prevailing in dire and dangerous times. The Way of Men is a tactical ethos.

If you are fighting to stay alive and you are surrounded by potential threats, what do you need from the men fighting with you?

What do you need from *us* to fend off *them*?

If eating means facing danger together, who do you want to take with you?

What virtues do you need to cultivate in yourself and the men around you to be successful at the job of hunting and fighting?

When your life and the lives of people who you care about depend on it, you'll need the men around you to be as strong as they can be. Living without the aid of advanced technology requires strong backs and elbow grease. You'll need strong men to fight off other strong men.

You won't want the men in your gang to be reckless, but you'll need them to be courageous when it matters. A man who runs when the group needs him to fight could put all of your lives in jeopardy.

You'll want men who are competent, who can get the job done. *Who wants to be surrounded by morons and fuck-ups?* The men who hunt and fight will have to demonstrate mastery of the skills your group uses to hunt and fight. A little inventiveness couldn't hurt, either.

You'll also need your men to commit. You will want to know that the men beside you are *us* and not *them*. You'll need to be able to count on them in times of crisis. You want guys who have your back. Men who don't care about what the other men think of them aren't dependable or trustworthy. If you're smart, you will want the other men to prove they are committed to the team. You'll want them to show that they care about their reputation within the gang, and you'll want them to show that they care about your gang's reputation with other gangs.

Strength, Courage, Mastery, and Honor.

These are the practical virtues of men who must rely on one another in a worst-case scenario. Strength, Courage, Mastery, and Honor are simple, functional virtues. They are the virtues of men who must answer to their brothers first, whether their brothers are good or unscrupulous men. These tactical virtues point to triumph. They are amoral, but not immoral. Their morality is primal and it lives in a closed circle. The tactical virtues are unconcerned with abstract moral questions of universal right or wrong. What is right is what wins, and what is wrong is what loses, because losing is death and the end of everything that matters.

Strength, Courage, Mastery, and Honor are the virtues that protect the perimeter; they are the virtues that save *us*. These are the virtues that men need to protect their interests, but also the virtues they must develop to go after what they want. They are the virtues of the defender and the attacker. Strength, Courage, Mastery, and Honor belong to no one god, though many gods claim them. Whatever men fight for, Strength, Courage, Mastery, and Honor are what they must demand of each other if they are going to win.

Strength, Courage, Mastery, and Honor are the *alpha* virtues of men all over the world. They are the fundamental virtues of men because without them, no "higher" virtues can be entertained. You need to be alive to philosophize. You can add to these virtues and you can create rules and moral codes to govern them, but if you remove them from the equation altogether you aren't just leaving behind the virtues that are specific to men, you are abandoning the virtues that make civilization possible.

The men who are strong, courageous, competent and loyal will be respected and honored as valuable members of team "us."

Men who are exceptionally weak or fearful can't be counted on. Men who are inept in some important way must either find a way to compensate—and they will try if they are loyal and honorable, if they *want* to help with the hunting and fighting—or find other work to do in the tribe. A man of questionable loyalty, who doesn't seem to care what the other men think of him or how their tribe is perceived, will not be trusted by the hunting and fighting gang. Men who are not up to the job of fulfilling the first role of men for one or all of these reasons will be pushed out of the hunting and fighting group and sent to work with the women, the children, the sick and the elderly.

Men have different drives, aptitudes and temperaments. Most men have the ability to adapt to the hunting and fighting role, to life at the edge of the perimeter, but some men won't be able to cut it. They will be regarded as less manly and thought of as lesser men. Some men are going to get their feelings hurt. That's not fair, but *fairness is a luxury* that men can ill afford in dire times.

Men who want to avoid being rejected by the gang will work hard and compete with each other to gain the respect of the male gang. Men who are stronger, more courageous and more competent by nature will compete with each other for higher status within that group. As long as there is something to be gained by achieving a higher position within the gang — whether it is greater control, greater access to resources or just peer esteem and the comfort of being higher in the hierarchy than the guys at the bottom — men will compete against each other for a higher position. However, because humans are cooperative hunters, the party-gang principle scales down to the individual level. Just as groups of men will compete against each other but unite if they believe more can be gained through cooperation, individual men will compete within a gang when there is no major external threat but then put aside their differences for the good of the group. Men aren't wired to fight *or* cooperate; they are wired to fight *and* cooperate.

Understanding this ability to perceive and prioritize different levels of conflict is essential to understanding The Way of Men and the four tactical virtues. Men will constantly shift gears from in-group competition to competition between groups, or competition against an external threat.

It is good to be stronger than other men within your gang, but it is also important for your gang to be stronger than another gang. Men will challenge their comrades and test each other's courage, but in many ways this intragroup challenging prepares men to face intergroup competition. Just as it is important for men to show their peers they won't be pushed around, the survival of a group can depend on whether or not they are willing to push back against other groups to protect their own interests. Men love to show off new skills and find ways to best their pals, but mastery of many of the same skills will be crucial in battles with nature and other men. The sports and games men play most demand the kind of strategic thinking and/or physical virtuosity that would be required in a survival struggle. A man's reputation may keep men in his group from messing with him, and a group's reputation may make its enemies think twice about creating animosity.

Sociologists and street gang experts typically write about an excessive concern with reputation or a desire to avenge "disses" with confused, haughty contempt. But the truth is that men have behaved this way for most of human history, and the strategic reasons why should be obvious to anyone who doesn't feel he can rely on police protection. If no one is coming to save you, you'd better be tough or look tough, and you'll probably want some tough guys ready and willing to get your back.

I have no idea how people manage to be confused about something that simple and obvious, but I'm pretty sure our ancestors would have killed them and taken their stuff.

💀   💀   💀

The next four chapters will elaborate on what I mean by Strength, Courage, Mastery and Honor. These simple words have many meanings, and they mean different things to different people. The manly virtues represent concepts so universally appealing that even the weak, cowardly, inept, and dishonorable struggle to find ways in which they too can feel that they embody these virtues. With each of the four, I will show why they relate specifically to men, how women fit into the picture, and how the virtues relate to each other. Some of the virtues also have multiple aspects worth parsing out.

After we have examined each of the tactical virtues and considered them amorally, I'll address issues of morality and ethics again, and explain what I think the difference is between being a good man and being good at being a man—and why they're not the same thing.

STRENGTH

If you take a thing apart or modify it, there are certain aspects which must remain intact or be replaced for it to retain its identity. Without certain parts, it becomes something else.

Without strength, masculinity becomes something else — a different concept.

Strength is not an arbitrary value assigned to men by human cultures. Increased strength is one of the fundamental biological differences between males and females. Aside from basic reproductive plumbing, greater strength is one of the most prominent, historically consequential and consistently measurable physical differences between males and females.

It is fashionable today to put the word "weaker" in quotations to avoid offending women when they are referred to as the "weaker" sex. Quotation marks will not alter the basic human truth that men are still on average significantly physically stronger than women. Serious people should be able to admit that something is generally true when it is a verifiable fact. There is no good reason to be coy about it.

Strength isn't the only quality that matters. Sometimes it doesn't matter at all. Strength is rarely a disadvantage. However, in our mechanically-assisted modern world, physical strength is often less consequential than it used to be. Of consequence or not, it is what it is.

Women can demonstrate strength, but strength is a quality that defines masculinity. Greater strength *differentiates* men from women. Weak men are regarded as less manly, but no one really cares or notices if a woman is physically weaker than her peers. In a way this is truer—or truer across classes—than it ever has been. Women living on farms (or in primitive hunter-gatherer societies) were expected to do far more demanding physical labor than any work required of the average woman today.

We admire strength in female athletes, but a beautiful woman who can't lift a bag of groceries will still have many admirers and plenty of men will be willing to help carry her groceries. Many female celebrities who are considered beautiful by both men and women are so thin that they look starved and brittle. Collectively, we don't care whether a woman is strong or not. A woman is not considered less womanly if she is physically weak.

Many may consider a woman less womanly if she is too strong. Specifically, a woman tends to look more like a man if she has a conspicuously high level of muscle mass and unusually low body fat. Precisely because of the physiological differences between males and females, only the most dedicated and disciplined female bodybuilders ever manage to look like He-Man action figures with Barbie doll heads. Average women who train with weights will increase strength and overall health, but most will still look like women. Testosterone may or may not play an important role in female muscular development.[1] However, in men, testosterone—the

---

    1   Chee, Rosie. "Breaking the Myth: Increasing Testosterone In Females = Muscle Accretion, Strength Gains, And Fat Loss."*Bodybuilding.com.* 15 Oct. 2009. Web. 11 July 2011. http://www.bodybuilding.com/fun/myth-of-women-lifting-heavy2.htm

most recognized androgen—has a complementary relation-ship with increased strength and muscle mass. Men who have more muscle tend to have and maintain higher testosterone levels, and men who have higher testosterone levels tend to have an easier time getting bigger and stronger. Men who in-crease their testosterone levels—either through training and diet or via artificial means—tend to look *more* masculine. Put differently, men with more muscle look less like most women, and more like the least androgynous men. This has absolutely nothing to do with culture. There is no human culture where men who are weak are considered manlier while women who are more muscular are considered more womanly. The im-portance of strength varies from society to society (usually in some relationship to available technologies and the kind of work that is required of average people) but strength has been a masculinity defining quality always and everywhere.

If we are making an honest attempt to understand and define masculinity or manliness[2] as that which pertains to or is characteristic of men, physical strength must figure promi nently in that definition. The Way of Men is the Way of the Strong—or at least the *stronger*.

As I and many others have mentioned, strength is not always a great advantage in the modern world. However, if we go back to our primal gang—our band of brothers fight-ing for survival—the value of strength to the group increases substantially. Where there is work and fighting to be done, the advantages of being stronger are obvious. A man who can hit twice as hard is also, other variables aside, worth more to the gang. In addition to giving a man the ability to *take* a

---

2   I use these terms interchangeably, as I believe average people do. There is an orthodoxy in academia that prefers to make a distinction between masculinity and manliness, and this distinction serves the ideology of femi-nists and cultural determinists. For more on this debate, Harvey C. Mansfield outlined his reasons for writing about manliness instead of masculinity in his 2006 book, *Manliness*.

position of greater prominence in a gang, strength made him more valuable overall. A man who can carry twice as much as another man, other variables aside, is worth more to the gang.

One evolutionary biologist recently suggested that humans stood up because standing up gave human males a greater mechanical advantage when clobbering each other.[3] They may have started walking upright for other reasons as well. On a long enough timeline, "both A and B" is a reasonable explanation, if both explanations are reasonable. As a natural advantage, pummeling power matters. It is also generally believed that fighting is one of the reasons why males have greater upper body strength than females. In the primal gang, the man who is substantially stronger than all of his peers is a juggernaut *capable* of crushing everyone in his path. He is *capable* of exerting his *will* in any way he sees fit. (The will itself is our second manly virtue.)

Strength, in the strictest physical sense, is the muscular ability to exert pressure.

Putting aside the workings of involuntary muscles, for conscious beings strength is the ability to exert force in accordance with one's will. This can be as simple as forcing one bone toward another and releasing it. A certain amount of strength is required to wiggle your finger.

Strength is an aptitude. Strength is an ability that can be developed, but as with intelligence, most people will have a certain natural range of potential beyond which they will be unable to progress. Some individuals will have a greater

---

3   Maffly, Brian. "U. biologist argues humans stood up to fight, not walk." *Salt Lake Tribune* 18 May 2011. Web. 11 July 2011. http://www.aho-rautah.com/sltrib/news/51831880-78/carrier-males-humans-standing.html. csp?page=1

aptitude for developing strength than others. Humans
unequal in their aptitudes. This is one of the cruel but fundamental truths of human life.

It takes a certain amount of strength to reach for a piece
of fruit and yank it away from a plant. Strength is required to
build and to farm and to hunt and to carry groceries from the
store and put them in your car. Ask an old person if loss of
strength has impacted their lives in a negative or positive way.
A weaker person is more vulnerable. Less strength means it
is less likely that you will be able to push someone away who
wants to take something from you, and on a strictly physical level, reduced strength means a diminished ability to take
what you want from someone else. A person who is too weak
simply cannot survive. It is strength that makes all other values possible.

**Strength is the *ability* to exert one's will over oneself,
over nature and over other people.**

As we move from the dire circumstances of the survival
gang to luxurious life in a civilized society, the concept of
strength doesn't change so much as it expands and becomes
a metaphor. The word strength can describe a wide range of
abilities and powers without losing its primal meaning or ca-
chet. Strength is the corporeal equivalent of power. Strength
is having 300 tanks to use against your enemy's 200 tanks.
Strength is the arsenal, but no guarantee that the arsenal will
be used. Strength, in this broader sense, is a desirable com-
modity. Getting stronger—increasing strength—means increasing your ability, as an individual, a gang or a nation, to
do as you wish with relative impunity. What is freedom, if
not the ability to do what one wishes?

Strength is the ability to move, and greater strength moves
more. However, just as muscles can make isometric contrac-
tions, strength can also be the ability to stand against outside
pressure. Strength is also the ability to HOLD FAST—a tat-

too once found on the knuckles of sailors whose lives (and the lives of the gang of men on their ship) depended on their ability to hold on and weather a storm. That strength means both the ability to move and the ability to become immovable is no more a contradiction than the mechanics of a muscle are a contradiction.

Physical strength is the defining metaphor of manhood because strength is a defining characteristic of men. An increased aptitude for physical strength differentiates most males from most women, and this difference, though less important in times of safety and plenty, has defined the role of men for all of human history.

Strength can be put to a variety of uses, but when it is put to no use, it is like a powerful engine collecting dust in a garage or a beautiful singing voice that no one ever hears. A sports car that never puts rubber to the road is just a pretty hunk of metal. To experience the joy of his natural talent, a singer must sing. The experience of being male is the experience of having greater strength, and strength must be exercised and demonstrated to be of any worth. When men will not or cannot exercise their strength or put it to use, strength is decorative and worthless.

COURAGE

Strength is a straightforward, physical concept.

Courage has many names, and has been defined in many ways.

Strength is the ability to move or stand against external forces. Courage is kinetic. Courage initiates movement, action or fortitude. Courage exercises strength. The "cowardly lion"—the tough looking guy who stands aside as weaker men fight the fight, take the risks and do the work— is worth less than the men who step into the arena.

I will not claim that all exertions of will are courageous, but all acts which require courage are exertions of will. It does not take courage to use strength to pick up a glass and lift it to your mouth. Courage implies a risk. It implies a potential for failure or the presence of danger. Courage is measured against danger. The greater the danger, the greater the courage. Running into a burning building beats telling off your boss. Telling off your boss is more courageous than writing a really mean anonymous note. Acts without meaningful consequences require little courage.

Aristotle believed that courage was concerned with fear, and that while there were many things to fear in life, death was the most fearful thing of all. In his *Nicomachean Ethics*, the brave man is a man who, "is fearless in the face of a noble death, and all of the emergencies that involve death; and the emergencies of war are in the highest degree of this kind." He also made the point that men who are forced to fight are less courageous than those who demonstrate courage in battle of their own free will. Aristotle framed courage as a moral virtue, as a will to noble action. He questioned the courage of those who are confident due to success in battle, though I wonder how such success can be earned, except through some initial show of courage. While it is true that the chests of strong and experienced men often swell when threats are minor, and such men have been known to back down in the face of a legitimate challenge, a certain amount of courage is the product of a successful track record. Is a man who has never won a fight more courageous for taking on an experienced fighter—no matter how noble the cause—or is he simply a fool? Aristotle's mean of courage is not the wild, "rash" confidence of a passionate man who fights in the heat of the moment out of fear or anger. Rather, he suggests that "brave men act for honor's sake, but passion aids them." He does allow that men who act from strength of feeling possess "something akin to courage." [1] Aristotle's formulation of courage, while admirable, is so conditional and lashed to a slippery, high-minded ideal of noble action that trying to determine who is truly courageous becomes a bit of a game.

Andreia, the word Aristotle used for courage, was also synonymous with manliness in ancient Greece. *Andreia* is derived from "andros," which connotes "male" or "masculine." In his book *Roman Manliness*, classicist Myles McDowell ar-

---

1   *The Nichomachean Ethics*. Trans. David Ross. Oxford World's Classics ed. N.p.: Oxford University Press, 1998. 63-73. Print.

gued that the word *virtus*,[2] which "struck the ear of an ancient Roman much as 'manliness' does that of an English speaker,"[3] meant courage—specifically in battle—in pre-Classical Latin. The word *vir* meant "man," and the *virtus* meant courage.[4] McDonnell wrote:

> "In military contexts *virtus* can denote the kind of courage required to defend the homeland, but more often it designates aggressive conduct in battle. In non-military situations courageous *virtus* usually refers to the capacity to face and endure pain and death."[5]

Courageous manliness is personified in the story of Gaius Mucius, a noble Roman youth from the early Republic. An Etruscan king named Porsenna had besieged Rome by garrisoning his soldiers around the city. Gaius Mucius asked the Roman senators for permission to slip into the Etruscan camp and kill Porsenna. He killed Porsenna's secretary by mistake, and he was captured by the king's bodyguards. Gaius Mucius said to the king:

---

2   It is from the Latin word *virtus* that we get the English word "virtue." This is due to the expansion of the concept of *virtus* in the later stages of the Roman Empire, where it absorbed a wider range of other values and became a kind of "moralized masculinity." McDonnell's thesis was that this was not always so, and he provided numerous examples from early Roman literature and records to prove that the early Romans equated *virtus* ("manliness") with martial valor.

3   McDonnell, Myles. *Roman Manliness : Virtus and the Roman Republic.* Cambridge University Press, 2006. 4. Print.

4   Ibid. 12.

5   Ibid. 31.

> "I am Gaius Mucius, a citizen of Rome. I came here as an enemy to kill my enemy, and I am as ready to die as I am to kill. We Romans act bravely and, when adversity strikes, we suffer bravely. Nor am I the only one who feels this way; behind me stands a line of those who seek the same honour."[6]

Porsenna threatened to throw Gaius Mucius into the fire. Gaius Mucius responded by thrusting his own hand into the fire. As his hand burned, he said:

> "Look upon me and realize what a paltry thing the body is for those who seek great glory."[7]

Porsenna told Gaius Mucius that, were he a member of his own tribe, he would commend him for his bravery. Gaius Mucius was released, but he told Porsenna that there were three hundred other Romans who would be willing to sacrifice themselves as he had to save their city, and that if the siege of Rome persisted, sooner or later one of them would manage to succeed in killing the king. Porsenna sent an envoy to the Romans, offering peace terms. Gaius Mucius earned the nickname "Scaevola," meaning "left-handed," after losing his right hand to the fire.

For both Aristotle and the Romans, courage—and manliness—was the will to heroically risk life and limb against a danger to the people of one's own tribe, especially in the context of war with another tribe. Aristotle's most noble form of courage was a willingness to take a necessary risk to ensure

---

6   Livy. *The Rise of Rome*: Books One to Five (Bks. 1-5) Book 2: 12. (Kindle Locations 1482-1484). Kindle.

7   Ibid.

the survival of the group. A demonstration of the willingness to risk one's own being for the gang proves loyalty and increases a man's value to the gang. When the chips are down, a man who shows this kind of courage can be counted on to give everything he has—even sacrificing himself—for the survival of the group. When a group is not facing a survival challenge, that group can afford to be metaphorical about courage and acknowledge lesser sacrifices. Until security is established, though, no group can afford to bother with niceties like "intellectual courage."

The word courage is used cheaply today. Any celebrity who gets sick and doesn't spend every day crying about it is lauded by tabloids for his or her "courageous battle" with cancer or chronic fatigue syndrome or depression or even "food addiction." There is nothing wrong with acknowledging the difficulties others face, but we can also acknowledge, as Aristotle and the Romans did, that courage in its highest and purest form involves the willful risk of bodily harm or death for the good of the group. Lesser risks require greater dilutions of courage.

Aristotle believed that heroic courage was the noblest form of moral courage, but he also noted that passion, spiritedness was "something akin to courage." In Plato's *Republic*, it is suggested that savage cruelty comes from the same part of man that inspires acts of great courage.[8] Courage was a trained, mature, socially aware and cooperative form of spirit. Translator Allan Bloom identified the raw form of courage— *thumos*[9] or "spiritedness"—as "the principle or seat of anger or rage."[10] Socrates likened the guardians of his city to "noble

---

8   *Republic*. Trans. Allan Bloom. Basic Books, 1968. 89. Print. (Book 3: 410d-e)

9   Also transliterated "thymos." θύμος.

10   *Republic*. Trans. Allan Bloom. Basic Books, 1968. 449. Print. (Notes, Book 2: 33)

puppies," who would be gentle with the people they knew but be eager to fight ferociously against strangers and outsiders when necessary.[11]

To get at the essence of what masculinity really is, let's remove the gilding of morality and nobility for a moment. While I do believe that some men demonstrate heroic tendencies at an almost instinctive level—like noble puppies—I will also say that before a man can be willing to take a risk for the group, he must be willing to take risks generally. Some men and women are described as being "risk-averse," and will go out of their way to avoid almost any kind of risk at all. Before we can have a willingness to take risks for the group— call that "high courage"—we must also possess some kind of "low courage" that amounts to a comfort with risk-taking. Risk-taking comes more naturally to some than to others, and it comes more naturally to men than it does to women. [12] As strength is trainable, so is courage. But like strength, some have a greater aptitude for risk-taking than others. Males socialize each other—hell, they *taunt* and *goad* each other gleefully—into taking risks. When there is no heroic objective in sight, boys will dare each other to do all sorts of stupid things. However, a male who is comfortable with low risk taking is likely going to be surer of himself—and more successful— when the time comes to take a heroic risk.

When answering the question "what is masculinity?" it is also important to keep sight of the individual within the group. Heroic courage benefits the group, but as we have discussed there are benefits to gaining status within the group and men will fight for that status. This requires a less noble

---

11   *Republic*. Trans. Allan Bloom. Basic Books, 1968. 52. Print. (Book 2: 373-376)

12   Kruger, Daniel J. "Sexual selection and the Male:Female Mortality Ratio." *Evolutionary Psychology* 2 (2004): 66-85. Web. 11 Aug. 2011. http:// www.epjournal.net/filestore/ep026685.pdf

kind of courage. It requires a spiritedness on one's own behalf. The strength of man is not merely a tool to be used in
the service of others. Men also use strength to advance their
own interests and it is foolish to expect them to make endless
sacrifices without personal gain of some kind, be it material
or spiritual. We should expect men to fight for themselves, to
compete with one another and to look after their own interests. Nothing could be more natural than a man who wants to
triumph and prosper.

It is not the strongest man who will necessarily lead, it
is the man who *takes* the lead who will lead. This intragroup
courage is required for a man to assert his interests over the
interests of other men within the group. At the most primal
level, asserting your interests over the interests of another
man requires a potential threat of violence. This is how men
have always sized each other up, and this is how they size
each other up today. This base, amoral courageous spirit is
required to move ahead of other men within a hierarchy. It's
the essence of competitive spirit. Nose-to-nose, men still look
each other over and try to perceive whether—and to what
extent—another man would be willing to press his interests.

If I push, will he give way? Will he push back?

This basic "push" is the spark of courage. If it isn't sufficiently present in a man, I doubt higher forms of courage
would even be possible. There are many names for the kind of
courage required to take risks to advance one's own interests.
Most people would call it *balls*.

Another word is "gameness." Sam Sheridan wrote about
it in *A Fighter's Heart*. Gameness is a term used in dogfighting
to describe, "the eagerness to get into the fight, the berserker
rage, and then the absolute commitment to the fight in the
face of pain, of disfigurement, until death."

In dogfighting, two dogs will fight until they are broken
up for some reason. The dogs will be pulled back behind

"scratch lines" in their corners and released. Dogs who jump back into the fight—this is called "making scratch"—are said to be "game." Dogfighting is a test of this gameness. According to Sheridan, dogfighting is not meant to be a fight to the death. The dogs fight until one of them refuses to cross the scratch lines and continue the fight.[13] It's like tapping out or saying "uncle."

Men evaluate each other for gameness, and this is the reason it was relevant in Sheridan's book about amateur and professional fighting. This indomitable spirit is a major theme in every heroic journey. In sports, it's part of the comeback tale. A guy faces his toughest challenge and then, when all but a few have counted him out, he comes back—running on pure "heart"—and triumphs over his opponent. It's the climax of every Rocky story and it was a gimmick in most of Hulk Hogan's professional wrestling matches. In every *Die Hard* movie, John McClane manages to save the day only after he's been beaten and bruised and comes back from the brink of defeat. These heroes have a push inside that keeps them coming back again and again after others would have given up.

A man who is obviously game can step ahead of a man who is not, simply because he can expect the man who is less game to yield to him. Some people talk about masculinity by attempting to determine who is "alpha" and who is "beta" in

---

13   Sheridan, Sam. *A Fighter's Heart : One Man's Journey Through the World of Fighting*. Grove Press, 2007. 280. Print.

a given situation.[14] A good friend put it to me this way: "If you can treat another man like he is your kid brother, you are the alpha."[15] The alpha will be the man with more push, and he will push ahead of the beta.

Feigning gameness can be an effective strategy, so long as no one calls your bluff. Gameness can be feigned through body language, through vocal inflection and through word choice. Creating a sense that you are ready to push as hard as necessary to get what you want is a way to establish authority, whether you are a prisoner, a businessman, a law enforcement professional, a parent or someone trying to discipline a dog. Most people will not test someone who is feigning gameness if the actor is convincing enough. Feigning gameness is a means of asserting one's will, and people do it all the time even in primitive societies. Failed attempts to feign gameness—trying to look tougher than you are, and not pulling it off—are what feminists point to when they talk about "performing masculinity" or putting on a "tough guise." What they are recognizing is the fact that men today still go through the ritual of establishing hierarchies and sizing each other up, even though most are untested and few will ever fight. It can seem silly to watch precisely because it is divorced from the deadly serious tactical reality of a survival scenario.

Feigning gameness can also unfortunately lead to delusional behavior. Many people affect the attitudes and postures of violence even though they have no experience with or

---

14   This is a common topic in the "manosphere" and the "game" community. I do not believe that alphas and betas are fixed types. I use these labels (as I have above) to describe dominant and submissive relationships between given sets of men. A man can be near the top of one hierarchy and near the bottom in another. One man's alpha can be another man's beta. This makes sense in our primate-based gang model, where members test each other and change roles. Even insular hierarchies shift, and the male on top today may not be in charge tomorrow.

15   h/t Max.

expectation of physical violence. There is a fearlessness that comes with knowing you can say whatever you want because there is a large, heavily armed man standing behind you. People can talk tough without having to do the primitive math of violence, because they believe that law enforcement will either intervene and stop or punish an attacker. Delusional gameness relies on the deterrent of men and women who are prepared to use violence to enforce the law. Delusional gameness is only possible when there is almost no danger of violent escalation. In less secure, less luxurious times and places, assertiveness must be accompanied by physical courage and daring. When there is no expectation that you will be "saved" or that most people fear the violent retribution of the state, it is foolish to provoke a dangerous looking man unless you are prepared to fight him.

The raw courage of gameness may correlate with the surety of greater size and strength to some degree, but many smaller men are as game as or more game than their larger counterparts. Flyweight fighters are a good example of men who are extremely game, though they are far less strong than many larger men who are less game. Weight-classed combat sports show that men of all sizes can demonstrate terrific gameness.

Both men and women can be game, but status for human females has rarely depended on a woman's willingness to fight. Demure, polite, passive women are attractive to men and are generally well-liked by other women. Even today, many men will jump at the opportunity to harm a man who harms a female stranger. Because of this, many women can be assertive or make displays of gameness with relative impunity, and some become delusional about their ability to make good on their threats or defend themselves if their taunts result in violence.

Gravitas is another old word that we still use to talk about manliness, especially in actors and politicians. We say a man possesses *gravitas* when he makes us believe we should take him seriously. We get our word "gravity" from the Latin *gravitas*; it means "heavy." The Romans used *gravitas* the same way we do—to say that a man or a thing is to be taken seriously. Contrasted with the frenzied imagery of a game pit bull, it balances out our sense of what manly courage is. Courage is not only the desire to leap into battle or move up in a hierarchy, it is also about defending position. Masculine men make it clear that they are to be taken seriously, that they have weight, that they won't be pushed around. Men want other men to know that they will be "heavy" to move, and must be taken seriously.

Courage is the animating spirit of masculinity, and it is crucial to any meaningful definition of masculinity. Courage and strength are synergetic virtues. An overabundance of one is worth less without an adequate amount of the other. In any gang of men fighting for survival, courage will be esteemed and respected in the living and it will be revered in the dead. Courage is a crucial tactical value. One can choose to be courageous, and even in its basest form, courage is a triumph over fear. It's associated with heart and spirit and passion, but it is also a drive to fight and win.

Courage is abstract, and it has many aspects, so I have summarized its definition as it relates to our attempt to understand The Way of Men and the gang ethos.

Courage is the *will* to risk harm in order to benefit oneself or others. In its most basic amoral form, courage is a willingness or passionate desire to fight or hold ground at any cost (gameness, heart, spirit, *thumos*). In its most developed, civilized and moral form courage is the considered and decisive willingness to risk harm to ensure the success or survival of a group or another person (courage, *virtus, andreia*).

Comparing his own experiences as a fighter to watching dogs fight, Sam Sheridan wrote:

> "They writhe furiously like snakes, twisting and spitting and slavering, growling like bears. Fury epitomized. Their tails are wagging, this is what they are meant to do, and they're fulfilling their purpose, they're *becoming*. There is blood, but the dogs don't care, turning and pinning, fighting off their backs and then clawing their way to standing [..] any pain they feel is overwhelmed by the desire to get the other dog. I know that feeling."

Plato (or Socrates) also compared men to dogs. One of the great tragedies of modernity is the lack of opportunity for men to become what they are, to do what they were bred to do, what their bodies want to do. They could be Plato's noble puppies, but they are chained to a stake in the ground—left to the madness of barking at shadows in the night, taunted by passing challenges left unresolved and whose outcomes will forever be unknown.

MASTERY

Men have always recognized themselves in animals. They have worshipped animals and claimed totemic lineage from animals. Men have traced their origins to gods who were like animals, part animal, or who could change into animals. Heracles was depicted wearing the skin of a powerful lion he killed. Norse berserkers wore the skins of wolves and bears to intimidate their enemies and inspire ferocious courage in battle. In the Aztec military, it was the elite Jaguar Warriors who went to the front. Military units and sports teams around the word adopt the names of formidable animals to represent their own gameness and strength.

Throughout this book, I have compared men to dogs and to chimpanzees. However, in sport and in war and in life, there is another manly virtue that is universally and specifically human because for the most part it requires human intellect.

Animals succeed or fail largely due to a combination of their circumstances and their inborn genetic fitness for a given situation. An animal who is stronger, nimbler or more game will triumph over an inferior animal. We have to project our own humanity onto animals to make them masters of strategy. In all but the most intelligent animals like higher primates and orca or dolphins, what we read as skill is most often instinct—not the product of thinking or tinkering or trial and error. The desire and ability to use reason and to develop skills and technologies that allow one to gain mastery over one's circumstances—over oneself, over nature, over other men, over women— is a human virtue, although it is also man's Achilles heel.

If you ask men what it means to be good at being a man, you'll often get answers that start to sound like a set of minimum skill proficiencies in a job description.

While the job description for men undeniably changes according to time, place and culture, the primal gang virtue that unifies them all is "being able to carry your own weight."

Women are more comfortable with accepting the benevolent aid of the group because they have always required it. A healthy adult woman must accept aid from the group if she is to carry a child, give birth and care for an infant. And, especially when men have achieved a level of security and prosperity beyond mere survival, women have been evaluated by men based less on their utility than on more nebulous qualities like attractiveness and social charm. When they have the means, most men will happily support a woman who seems to be carefree, pretty and charming.

This has not been the case with men. It is far rarer for women or men to volunteer to support a grown, able-bodied man. It is rarer still for them to support him without resentment. There is no point in an adult male's life when he can be excused from carrying his own weight, except when he is sick, injured, handicapped or old. Human societies accommodate all of these exceptions, but competency has always been crucial to a man's mental health and sense of his own worth. Men want to carry their own weight, and they should be expected to. As Don Corleone might put it, women and children could afford to be careless for most of human history, but not men. Men have always had to demonstrate to the group that they could carry their own weight.

Until you can function as a competent member of the group and carry your own weight, you are a supplicant and a drag on the collective. A child is a child, but an incompetent adult is a beggar. One of the problems with massive welfare states is that they make children or beggars of us all, and as such are an affront and a barrier to adult masculinity. It has become clichéd comedy for men and women to laugh at men who are concerned with being competent. The "men refuse to stop and ask for directions" joke never seems to get old for women, who are more comfortable with dependence, or socialist types, because reducing men to a childlike state of supplication and submission to state bureaucrats is required for big-government welfare states to function. Masculine loathing of dependence is a bulwark to the therapeutic mother state.

Dependency is powerlessness. Yet, men have always been cooperative hunters, and in a survival scenario they will fall into hierarchies based on strength and gameness. Men have a certain natural comfort with interdependency. Claims of complete independence are generally bullshit. Few of us have ever survived or would be able to survive on our own for an extended period of time. Few of us would want to. A child is completely dependent and powerless. It has no control over its own fate. Controlling one's own fate within the context of group give-and-take has to do with figuring out what you bring to the table and making yourself valuable to the group. The bare minimum required for moving from dependence to interdependence is competence and self-sufficiency—the ability to carry one's own weight.

Becoming an interdependent, rather than completely dependent, member of the group means *mastering* a set of useful skills and understanding some useful ideas. We send children to school to master a set of skills and a body of knowledge that we think they'll need to carry their own weight in society and function as adults. Most militaries send men to boot camp. At boot camp, men learn a basic skill set and body of knowledge necessary to function within the military. Boot camp graduates can theoretically be expected to at least carry their own weight in an offensive or defensive scenario.

Understanding The Way of Men means understanding how men evaluate each other as men, and how they accord status to men within the context of a primal history common to all men. The amoral masculine gang ethos is tactical and utilitarian. It's kind of like picking men for a sports team. Before people care about whether or not you're a good person, they want to know if you're a good player. Speculating about the morality of professional athletes is a popular form of male social gossip, but when the athletes take the field, what matters most is how they can contribute to a team's success. Men want to know if they have the physical ability, the gameness and the mastery of the skills necessary to help the team *win.*

The Way of Men, the gang ethos, and the amoral tactical virtues are fundamentally about winning. Before you can have church and art and philosophy, you need to be able to survive. You need to triumph over nature and other men, or at the very least you need to be able to keep both at bay. Winning requires strength and courage, and it requires a sufficient mastery of the skills required to win.

Stated as a manly virtue:

Mastery is a man's desire and ability to cultivate and demonstrate proficiency and expertise in technics that aid in the exertion of will over himself, over nature, over women, and over other men.

Advanced levels of mastery and technics allow men to compete for improved status within the group by bringing *more* to the camp, hunt or fight than their bodies would otherwise allow. Mastery can be supplementary—a man who can build, hunt and fight, but who can also do something else well, be it telling jokes or setting traps or making blades, is worth more to the group and is likely to have a higher status within the group than a man who can *merely* build, hunt and fight well. Mastery can also be a compensatory virtue, in the sense that a weaker or less courageous man can earn the esteem of his peers by providing something else of great value. It could well have been a runt who tamed fire or invented the crossbow or played the first music, and such a man would have earned the respect and admiration of his peers. Homer was a blind man, but his words have been valued by men for thousands of years.

Women also earn their keep through mastery of one kind or another, and mastery is by no means exclusive to men, but mastery does have a lot to do with competition for status between men. If necessity is the mother of invention, it is the need to compete for status and peer esteem—to find a valued place in the group—that drives many inventors to invent. The drive to gain control over something is part of the drive to master nature.

Strength, courage, and honor make a tidy triad, because they are all directly concerned with violence. But the picture of how men judge men as men is incomplete without some concept of mastery. Strength, gameness, and competition for status are all present in animals, but it is the conscious drive to master our world that differentiates men from beasts. Whether you're a benevolent king or a ruthless gangster, a man with a special skill, talent or technology can be as valuable as or exponentially more valuable than your toughest thug. It is mastery more often than brute strength that allows the elite to rule. Masculinity can never be separated from its connection to violence, because it is through violence that we ultimately compete for status and wield power over other men. However, mastered skills and technology provide deciding advantages in fighting, hunting and surviving for human men.

HONOR

The idea of honor shines an ancient light so warm and golden that everyone wants to stand in it. This is the most natural desire in the world, because honor in its most inclusive sense is esteem, respect and status. To be honored is to be respected by one's peers.

Thomas Hobbes wrote in *Leviathan* that what was honorable was, "whatsoever possession, action, or quality, is an argument and a signe of Power."[1] Hobbes believed that honor existed in a free market, where value was accorded to men based on what men had to offer and the value that other men placed on it. For Hobbes, honor was a form of deference, an acknowledgement of power and influence over other men.

In our rudimentary gang of a few men depending on each other in a hostile environment, this definition of honor is directly related to the other three masculine virtues. In a hostile environment, strength, courage, and mastery are all absolutely necessary for survival and everyone in the gang understands this to be true because external threats are regular and imminent. Men who exhibit these traits will have greater

---

1   Hobbes, Thomas. *Leviathan*. 1651. Cambridge University Press, 1996. 65. Print.

value to the group and contribute more to the group's survival and prosperity. Deference acknowledges interdependency and loyalty.

In a relatively secure society, while power ultimately comes from the ability to use violence, there are so many middlemen involved that the person who wields the most power and influence may simply be the person with the most wealth or popularity. For instance, teen singing stars and talk show hosts can wield tremendous power and influence, but their power has little or nothing to do with the esteem of the fighting men who gave the word honor its heroic glow.

According to James Bowman, there are two types of honor. *Reflexive honor* is the primitive desire to hit back when hit, to show that you will stand up for yourself.

To expand on Bowman's theory, reflexive honor is the signal of the rattlesnake, communicating a reputation for retaliation summed up by the popular old motto *Nemo me impune lacessit,* or "No one attacks me with impunity." To protect one's honor is as defensive as it is offensive—even if attack is pre-emptive, as it often is. People are more likely to leave you alone if they fear harm from you, and if men give way to you because they fear you, you will gain a certain status among men. This is equally true for a group, and in a survival scenario it is generally a tactical advantage to appear to be fearsome. That is, it is tactically advantageous to cultivate a reputation for strength, willingness to fight and technical mastery.

A man once said, "If I allow a man to steal my chickens, I might as well let him rape my daughters." That's reflexive honor.

Bowman also recognized the idea of *cultural honor*, which he defined as a sum of the "traditions, stories and habits of thought of a particular society about the proper and improper uses of violence."[2]

Bowman's definition of cultural honor has a moral cast to it. While Bowman links it to violence above, he notes throughout his book that there is a conflict, especially (but not uniquely) in the Western mind between manly public honor and private, moral honor that has as much to do with one's personal philosophy and a desire to be a good person as it does with one's reputation for violent retaliation in the eyes of men. While Bowman's view of cultural honor follows from reflexive honor, cultural honor is ultimately concerned with being a good man, not being good at being a man.

Because it is linked to morality and what is valued culturally, the cultural code of honor can morph into virtually anything. We see this in the way the blood is wiped from the blade of honor today. Honor is used to indicate almost any sort of general esteem, deference or respect. School recognition programs like The National Honor Society continue the meritocratic, hierarchical sense of honor—because study is an attempt at mastery—however gender-neutral and non-violent. The deference that Hobbes recognized in honor is now applied to abstract concepts that have little or nothing to do with traditional honor.

For instance, the slogan "Honor Diversity" is popular with gay rights advocates, who reject traditional, hierarchical ways of defining both honor and masculinity. "Honor Diversity" is an interesting slogan, because it essentially means "honor everyone and everything." If everyone is honored equally, and everyone's way of life is honored equally, honor

---

2   Bowman, James. *Honor : A History*. Encounter Books, 2006. 6. Print.

has no hierarchy, and therefore honor has little value according to the economics of supply and demand. "Honor diversity" doesn't mean much more than "be nice."

If honor is to mean anything at all, it must be hierarchical. To be honored, as Hobbes recognized, is to be esteemed, and as humans are differently-abled and differently motivated, some will earn greater esteem than others. Americans have a strained relationship with the idea of honor. They have always been a little drunk on the idea that "all men are created equal" and politicians have spent two centuries flattering every Joe Schmoe into thinking his opinion is worth just as much as anyone else's—even when he has absolutely no idea what he is talking about. American men profess the creed of equality, but if you put a bunch of American men in a room or give them a job to do, they work out their *Lord of the Flies* hierarchies in the same way that men always have. The religion of equality gives way to the reality of meritocracy, and there's not too great a leap between Geoffroi de Charny's motto "who does more is worth more" and the rugged individualism of the American who was expected to pull himself up "by his own bootstraps."

To honor a man is to acknowledge his accomplishments and recognize that he has attained a higher status within the group.

If we stop there and say that honor is merely high group status, we still have a definition of honor that would be unrecognizable to the knights, the samurai, the ancient Greeks, and the ancient Romans who—among many others—give the idea of honor the noble, mythic quality that makes it so appealing.

The reason for this is simple.

Honor has always been about the esteem of groups of men.

It probably never occurred to Hobbes to include this *caveat*, because despite the occasional female monarch, he lived his entire life in a system designed to favor male interests. The thought of a system where females had an equal say has been unthinkable to all but a few before our time. Men have always ruled, and men have always determined what behaviors were honored and what behaviors were considered dishonorable. And while the specifics of these honor codes have changed as circumstances and prevailing moralities changed, the majority of men still acknowledged the fundamental tactical necessity of reflexive honor. They still judged each other as men according to the basic masculine virtues of strength, courage and mastery.

When the word "honor" is connected to the word "culture" and framed as a negative, social scientists seem to be more comfortable with a definition of honor similar to the one I'm presenting here. Recently, an article linking a higher rate of accidental death in males to risk-taking and honor culture in southern states[3] received attention from mainstream news outlets.[4] The researchers in question defined this honor culture according to cultural emphasis on "the relentless, and sometimes violent, defense of masculine reputation, which is presumably a social adaptation to an environment characterized by scarce resources, frequent intergroup aggression (e.g., raiding), and the absence of the rule of law."[5] They hypoth-

---

3   Collin D. Barnes, Ryan Brown, and Michael Tamborski. "Living Dangerously: Culture of Honor, Risk-Taking, and the Nonrandomness of "Accidental" Deaths." *Social Psychological and Personality Science.* June 8, 2011 1948550611410440, first published on June 8, 2011. Online.

   http://spp.sagepub.com/content/early/2011/06/03/1948550611410440

4   Carollo, Kim. ""Honor Culture" Linked to Accidental Deaths." *http://abcnews.go.com.* ABC, 15 Aug. 2011. Web. 28 Aug. 2011.

   http://abcnews.go.com/Health/honor-culture-linked-higher-rate-accidental-deaths-south/story?id=14292632

5   Barnes *et al.*

esized that men from honor cultures would be more likely to engage in risky behaviors because "risky behaviors provide social proof of strength and fearlessness." While the study revealed the biases of its authors by focusing on the white honor culture of Southern Ulster-Scots and avoiding any discussion of honor cultures among Latino prison gangs, African warlords or Islamic terrorists, the researchers seemed to agree that honor among men tends to be defined by a concern with maintaining a reputation for strength and courage (two of our other three masculine virtues).

Bowman and others have written that "honor depends on the honor group."[6] The honor group is the male gang, and honor cultures are about status within a given gang of men. What the sociologists were essentially saying in their study of "honor states" is that some men care more about what other men think of them—specifically, their reputation for strength, honor and mastery—than others. Honor groups depend on a sense of shared identity. In a cosmopolitan scenario where frequent travel, fleeting connections and temporary alliances are the norm, the *us* vs. *them* never quite takes shape on the direct interpersonal level. Instead, the honor group is ritualized or metaphorical—as with sports teams and political parties and ideological positions. These allegiances can be abandoned easily, and personal accountability is minimal. Honor relies on face-to-face connections and the possibility of shame or dishonor in the eyes of other men. This partially explains why men who have grown up together in the same ghetto block or the same rural area, or who have spent time bunked together, will be more likely to be concerned with honor than more mobile men who travel a lot, or men who only spend time with other men in the presence of females.

As it relates to understanding the masculine ethos:

---

6   Bowman, James. *Honor : A History*. Encounter Books, 2006. 38. Print.

Honor is a man's reputation for strength, courage and mastery within the context of an honor group comprised primarily of other men.

Stated as a masculine virtue:

Honor is a *concern* for one's reputation for strength, courage and mastery within the context of an honor group comprised primarily of other men.

There are moral codes and cultural codes of honor that factor into men's estimation of the men within their honor groups, but the point here is to reduce masculinity to first principles without getting lost in a morass of variable cultural honor codes. What is common to the honor of the Mafioso and the honor of the knight, to the honor of American founding father Alexander Hamilton[7] and the honor of any naked savage is a concern for one's reputation as a man of strength, courage, and mastery, and how it relates to a man's sense of worthiness and belonging within the context of a male honor group.

UNDERSTANDING DISHONOR

Part of the reason that honor is a virtue rather than merely a state of affairs is that showing concern for the respect of your peers is a show of loyalty and indication of belonging — of being *us* rather than *them*. It is a show of deference. Hobbes noted that men honored each other by seeking each other's counsel and by imitating each other. Caring about what the men around you think of you is a show of respect, and conversely, not caring what other men think of you is a sign of disrespect.

---

7   Hamilton died from a wound suffered in a pistol duel with Vice President Aaron Burr in 1804.

In a survival band, it is tactically advantageous to maintain a reputation for being strong, courageous and masterful as a group. A man who does not care for his own reputation makes his team look weak by association. Dishonor and disregard for honor are dangerous for a survival band or a fighting team because the appearance of weakness invites attack. At the personal, intragroup level the appearance of weakness or submissiveness invites other men to assert their interests over your own.

The tactical problems presented by the appearance of weakness as a group explain, to some extent, the visceral response many men have to displays of flamboyant effeminacy. The word effeminacy is a bit misleading here, because this really *isn't* about women. The dislike of what is commonly called effeminacy is about male status anxiety and practical concerns about tactical vulnerabilities, and it is more accurate to discuss dishonor in terms of *deficient masculinity* and *flamboyant dishonor*.

***Deficient masculinity* is simply a lack of strength, courage or mastery.**

Because masculinity and honor are by nature hierarchical, all men are in some way deficient in masculinity compared to a higher status man. There is always a higher status man, if not in your group, then in another, and if not in this way then in that way, and if not now, then eventually. No one is the strongest, most courageous *and* the smartest or most masterful man—though some men are closer to the ideal or perfect "form" of masculinity than others. Masculinity in the perfect ideal is aspirational, not attainable. The point is to be better, stronger, more courageous, more masterful—to achieve greater honor.

The men who possess the least of these qualities or suffer from an excessive lack of one in particular are the men who other men don't want to be. They are furthest from the ideal.

So long as they don't openly despise the ideal or attempt to move the goalposts to appear "more masculine" by creating some new artificial standard, men will tend to include and help members of their gang or tribe who are unusually deficient in strength, courage or mastery. The lowest status men within a group are still usually included in the group unless they bring shame to the group as a whole—thus endangering the group, at least in theory—or fail so miserably that they become an excessive burden. Most high status men are not monsters, and most low status men don't want to be a burden on others (because dependency is slavery), so men who are not good at being men generally try to find some way to make themselves useful or at least tolerable to a given group of men. Think of the funny fat guys and the frail artists and the nurturing fellows who make sure everything is in order for the men of action. All large groups of men seem to have members who assume these kinds of low status roles while remaining part of the honor group.

Deficient masculinity is undesirable and results in low status. Men despise deficient masculinity in themselves because they would naturally rather be stronger, more courageous, and more masterful. Deficient masculinity rarely arouses *hate* or *anger* within a male group, though it may result in some general frustration.

FLAMBOYANT DISHONOR

Deficient masculinity is trying and failing. Failure is part of trying, and while men tease and goad each other, no man who has become masterful at anything has achieved that mastery without a certain amount of failure along the way.

Male groups are hierarchical, so while greater dominance is desirable, a certain amount of submission is essential to any co-operative group of men. Unless some men give way to others, you'll end up with too many chiefs and not enough Indians. Honor as a virtue means caring about what other men think of you, trying to earn their esteem, and asserting yourself as best you can to achieve the highest relative position within the group.

Flamboyant dishonor is not a failure of strength or courage. Men who are flamboyantly dishonorable are flagrant in their disregard for the esteem of their male peers. What we often call effeminacy is a theatrical rejection of the masculine hierarchy and manly virtues. Masculinity is religious, and flamboyantly dishonorable men are blasphemers. Flamboyant dishonor is an insult to the core values of the male group.

Flamboyant dishonor is an openly expressed lack of concern for one's reputation for strength, courage and mastery within the context of an honor group comprised primarily of other men.

In 1994, Michael Kimmel wrote an essay which provocatively asserted that "homophobia is a central organizing principle of our cultural definition of manhood." He went on to clarify that this homophobia had little or nothing to do with homosexual acts or an actual fear of homosexuals. He wrote, "Homophobia is the fear that other men will unmask us, emasculate us, reveal to the world that we do not measure up, that we are not real men. We are afraid to let other men see that fear."[8]

Why call it homophobia?

The kind of masculine status anxiety Kimmel wrote about has much to do with the way men fumble to translate the hon-

---

8   Michael, Kimmel S. "Masculinity as Homophobia." *Reconstructing Gender : A Multicultural Anthology.* Ed. Estelle Disch. 3rd ed. McGraw Hill, 2003. 103-09. Web. 8 Sept. 2011.

http://www.neiu.edu/~circill/F7587Z.pdf

or of the small, bonded male gang into a complex modern society full of mixed messages and overlapping male groups. This fear is a fear of the unknown. In an established, tightly bonded male group, men know about where they stand in the hierarchy. There's nowhere to hide, so there is less fear of being revealed as a fraud, and like some kind of primal sports ranking system, men are constantly tested against one another and against external forces.

I've observed this in the few brief introductions I've had to Brazilian *jiu-jitsu*, in gyms where everyone rolls with everyone. Men find out quickly who is good, and who isn't. There is no hiding or pretending and it doesn't matter whether or not your Internet profile picture looks tough or if you put on a good show—because here is this guy who is choking you out. You are revealed as what you are, and all that remains is to improve. The only way you can increase your status within the group is to try harder and get better.

Flamboyant dishonor is a little bit like walking into that room full of men who are trying to get better at *jiu-jitsu* and insisting that they stop what they are doing and pay attention to your fantastic new tap-dancing routine. The flamboyantly dishonorable man seeks attention for something the male group doesn't value, or which isn't appropriate at a given time.

At the primal level, flamboyant dishonor presents tactical problems for the group. By outwardly and theatrically rejecting the core masculine values, particularly strength and courage, the flamboyantly dishonorable male advertises weakness and a propensity for submission to outside watchers. Any honest student of human (and in many cases, primate) body language will be forced to recognize that the postures, gestures and intonations of males generally regarded as effeminate are in fact postures, gestures and intonations that communicate submissiveness. Humans are complicated, and when push comes to shove, stereotypically effeminate males are not always as submissive as their body language would seem to indicate. However, submissiveness is what they advertise.

This submissiveness correlates with male homosexuality, and the problems men have with male homosexuality—aside from concerns about unsolicited advances—are mostly related to the perception of an over-willingness to submit to other men. There are extremely submissive or flamboyantly dishonorable effeminate heterosexual men. Kimmel, for instance, is heterosexual but flamboyantly dishonorable. His wrists are limp, his gestures are airy, his demeanor is precious, and he has devoted his entire career to the open rejection of the manly virtues and a persistent devaluing of male honor codes. I do not need to insult him. None of these qualities are negative according to his own views, and I am certain he is proud of his life's work. He is a perfect example of a heterosexual male who flagrantly rejects the gang virtues of strength, courage, mastery, and honor.

The man who flamboyantly rejects the honor codes of the group can obviously not be trusted to "snap to" in a state of emergency. Dishonor is disloyalty. A man who not only openly refuses to strive to be as strong, courageous and competent as he can, but who flaunts these codes theatrically for all to see is a weak link. He makes his peers seem more vulnerable for tolerating vulnerability, and more cowardly for tolerating cowardice. He brings shame on the group, and with shame comes danger, because public displays of weakness and cowardice invite attack.

This tactical reasoning goes a long way toward explaining why men who function successfully within male honor groups make a big show of rejecting and distancing themselves from males who are flamboyantly dishonorable. By expelling effeminate males from the gang or by shaming them and pushing them to the fringes of a particular group, the group projects strength and unity. The group demonstrates that "we do not tolerate unmanly men here."

The shunning of homosexuals and perceived homosexuals is generally justified with appeals to divine or natural laws. That's spin that absolves men of responsibility for social cruelty to members of their own tribe. When men reject effeminate men they are rejecting weakness, casting it out, and cleansing themselves of its corrosive stigma.

In many societies that have openly tolerated effeminacy, flamboyantly effeminate males have been relegated to a half-man, half-woman status and given a special role. The Native American *berdake*, for example, were regarded as neither man nor woman. They were usually men, they dressed differently to distinguish themselves from men, they generally did what was considered woman's work within the village, and they were often regarded as serving a "mediating role between men and woman."[9] Indian *hijras* are another example of flamboyantly dishonorable (or gender non-conforming, if you prefer the feminist lingo) males who are accepted in society so long as they accept a special gender status and exist apart from normal men.

Honor is a powerful concept because it is connected to every man's primal need to demonstrate that he is of value to the group—that he is more of an asset than a liability. Women have a separate value to men and that has nothing to do with their ability to demonstrate strength, courage or mastery. Men who are deficient or handicapped in some way can deliver value in other ways. Most men care about being seen

9   Schnarch, Brian. "Neither Man nor Woman: Berdache — A Case for Non-Dichotomous Gender Construction." *Anthropologica*34.1 (1992): 105-21. *JSTOR*. Web. 8 Sept. 2011.

http://0-www.jstor.org.catalog.multcolib.org/stable/25605635

by other men as being strong, courageous and competent because these tactical virtues have been essential to their role as men and their very survival for most of human history. In a war or in an emergency, these virtues would still be of primary importance, and all other virtues would be comparatively incidental.

In less dire times, as opportunities for men to demonstrate the tactical virtues decrease, honor broadens its scope. Men still struggle to show other men that they are worthy. They still struggle to show that they are worth having around, worthy of belonging to the group—a valued member of "us." When there is less hunting and fighting to do, men attempt to increase their value to other men by showing that they are good people or good citizens—good members of the tribe. They try to show that they are good men. Earning and keeping a reputation as a good man overlaps conceptually with honor because it is another way to add value and show worth to other men. Honor as a virtue is a demonstration of group loyalty, so it naturally expands to include other demonstrations of loyalty to the values of the group—from piously praising the tribal gods to "standing up for what is right" according to the group's ethical codes.

Still, honor at is root is about showing men that you are good at being a man and good at filling man's first role on the perimeter. Showing other men that you are a good man is an outgrowth of that. Being a good man is related to honor, but it is not the root of honor. We care what other men think of us, first and foremost, because men have always depended on each other to survive. It is triumph over nature and triumph over other men—it is survival and prosperity and life itself— that give honor the golden glow which draws men to it and repels them from dishonor.

We see men of all kinds of professed creeds attain to almost all degrees of worth or worthlessness under any of them. This is not what I call religion, this profession and assertion; which is often only a profession and assertion from the outworks of the man, from the mere argumentative region of him, if even so deep as that. But the thing a man does practically believe (and this is often enough without asserting it even to himself, much less to others); the thing a man does practically lay to heart, and know for certain, concerning his vital relations to this mysterious Universe, and his duty and destiny there, that is in all cases the primary thing for him, and creatively determines all the rest. That is his religion; or, it may be, his mere skepticism and no-religion: the manner it is in which he feels himself to be spiritually related to the Unseen World or No-World; and I say, if you tell me what that is, you tell me to a very great extent what the man is, what the kind of things he will do is.

—Thomas Carlyle,

"On Heroes, Hero-Worship, and the Heroic in History"

ON BEING A GOOD MAN

Reducing masculinity to a handful of tactical virtues may seem crude, thuggish and uncivilized. What about moral virtue? What about justice, humility, charity, faith, righteousness, honesty, and temperance?

Aren't these manly virtues, too?

Men aren't heartless monsters and they aren't machines. Men think about more than hunting and killing and defending. Men are capable of compassion as well as cruelty.

Thinking men ask "why." It's not always enough to win. Men want to believe that they are *right*, and that their enemies are *wrong*. To separate *us* from *them*, men find moral fault in their enemies and create codes of conduct to distinguish themselves as good men. One of the finest examples of this is the Christian knight—an ascetic committed to piety and violence, fighting in shining armor for goodness with God on his side. Most men would agree that it is better to be a good man who stands up to bad men. They would rather be heroes than villains. Most men want to see themselves as good men fighting for something greater than survival or gain.

When you ask men about what makes a *real* man, a lot of them will get up on their high horses and start talking about what it means to be a *good* man.

"A real man would never hit a woman."

"A man who doesn't spend time with his family can never be a real man."

"A real man takes responsibility for his actions."

"A real man pays his debts."

"Real men love Jesus."

However, if you ask the same men to list their favorite "guy movies," many of them will include films like *The Godfather, Scarface, Goodfellas,* and *Fight Club*.

Don Corleone, Tommy DeVito, and Henry Hill were all ruthless racketeers. Scarface was a murdering drug lord. Tyler Durden was basically a domestic terrorist. There are scores of popular gang and heist flicks, among them: *Oceans 11* (and *12*, and *13*), *Snatch, Smoking Aces, The Italian Job, Heat, Ronin, The Sting, The Usual Suspects, Reservoir Dogs* and *Pulp Fiction*.[1] The calculating, morally ambiguous hitman for hire has found an especially sympathetic place in the cinematic pantheon of manliness: *The Professional, The Matador, In Bruges, The Mechanic, The American, Collateral, Road to Perdition, No Country for Old Men. Hitman* was both a film and a video game. Two of the best-selling video game franchises during the last decade were *Assassin's Creed* and *Grand Theft Auto. Sons of Anarchy,* a show about a motorcycle gang, is currently popular on television. Are its characters unmanly because they are outlaws? What about Tony from *The Sopranos* or Al Swearengen from *Deadwood*?

Was Darth Vader a pussy?

Despite the moral posturing, men are attracted to these characters precisely because they *are* manly. Bad guys tend

---

1   The author's favorite (Godfathers I & II exempted), is a British gangster flick: *The Long Good Friday* (1980)

to operate in brutal, indelicate, and unmoderated boys' clubs, and they seem to be *particularly* concerned with the business of being a man. Gangsters are status conscious, aggressive, tactically-oriented, ballsy, brother-bonded men's men. The loner hitmen are portrayed as capable but careful smooth operators who are masters of their dangerous craft. They are not good men, but they are good at doing the kinds of things that have been demanded of men throughout human history. They are not good men, but they are good at being men.

Before film, men and boys were thrilled by tales of outlaws, pirates, highwaymen, and thieves. Whether these stories were romanticized or spun as cautionary tales, they captured the male imagination with adventurous accounts of daring and mischievous virility.

In Shakespeare's *The Life of Henry the Fifth*, the King promised his enemies that unless they surrendered, his men would rape their shrieking daughters, dash the heads of their old men, and impale their naked babies on pikes. Today, if a military leader made a promise so indelicate, he would be fired and publicly denounced as an evil, broken psychopath. I can't call Henry an unmanly character with a straight face.

Consider also the case of the prisoner. Do you truly believe that men who negotiate a violent, all male world every day are less manly than a nice guy who works 9 to 5 in a cubicle farm and spends his free time doing whatever his wife tells him to do?

What about suicide bombers? I'd say that hijacking a plane with a box knife and flying it into a building takes *balls of steel*. I don't have to like it, but if I'm being honest with myself, I can't call those guys unmanly. Enemies of my tribe, yes. Unmanly, no. Remember that there are hundreds of thousands of men and boys who regard suicide bombers as brave, martyred heroes who took substantial risks and made the ultimate sacrifice for a cause. We think of them as *evil* and flatter ourselves by calling them *cowardly* because they aren't on our team, because they don't share all of our values, and because they endanger our collective interests.

We want our external enemies to be defective and unsympathetic. Many have written about our tendency to dehumanize our foes. Emasculating them is another aspect of that—it adds insult to injury. We also want to puff ourselves up and psych them out. It's good strategy. Insulting a man's honor— his masculine identity—is a good way to test him. It's a good way to get his blood up. It's a good way to pick a fight.

We want our villains within to be equally unsympathetic. Portraying bad men as unmanly men is a good way to dissuade young men from behaving badly. Making your own cultural heroes seem bigger than life men elevates group pride and morale. It makes sense to want your young men to emulate men who champion your people's values, and young men especially tend to choose the stronger horse.

Cultures have wrestled with the idea of what it means to be a good man for thousands of years. Waller R. Newell, a professor of political science and philosophy, collected a broad range of thinking on the topic for his book *What is a Man? 3,000 Years of Wisdom on the Art of Manly Virtue.* Newell criticized those who came of age in the 1960s for establishing a cultural orthodoxy prone to believing that "nothing just, good, or true" had happened before their time, and for causing the "disappearance of the positive tradition of manliness through relentless simplification and caricature."[2] He showed what he referred to as an "unbroken pedigree in the Western conception of what it means to be a man," which he defined as "honor tempered by prudence, ambition tempered by compassion for the suffering and the oppressed,

---

2   Newell, Waller R., ed. *What is a Man? 3,000 Years of Wisdom on the Art of Manly Virtue.* ReganBooks/HarperCollins, 2000. Print.

love restrained by delicacy and honor toward the beloved."[3] His sourcebook was filled with selections from Plato, Aristotle, Marcus Aurelius, Francis Bacon, Geoffrey Chaucer, William Shakespeare, Benjamin Franklin, Ralph Waldo Emerson, Winston Churchill, John F. Kennedy, and many others.

There is a movement to reclaim this idea of virtuous manhood—to show young men how to be good and manly men. In 2009, venture capitalist Tom Matlack started a "four-pronged effort to foster a discussion about manhood," called *The Good Men Project*. *The Good Men Project* currently exists as a foundation, an online magazine, a documentary film, and a book. The book is filled with stories of men who are struggling to be *good men* in the 21st Century, and trying to figure out what that means.

The Art of Manliness website was founded by Brett McKay and his wife Kate in 2008, and boasts some 90,000 subscribers.[4] The McKays have published two books offering their take on the subject of manliness: *The Art of Manliness – Classic Skills and Manners for the Modern Man*, and *The Art of Manliness - Manvotionals: Timeless Wisdom and Advice on Living the 7 Manly Virtues*. The site itself reveres good, manly historical figures like "Rough Rider" Theodore Roosevelt, and it has a nostalgic feel to it. It's a bit like a Boy Scout handbook for adult males, offering advice and "how to" articles to help out men who are trying to be good protectors, providers, husbands, and fathers. An *Art of Manliness* workout isn't just a workout; it becomes "hero training."

I asked Brett McKay about what he thought the difference was between being a good man and being good at being a man. He said that being good at being a man means, "being proficient in your ability to earn and keep your culture's idea

---

3   Ibid. XVIII.

4   "About Us." *The Art of Manliness*. Ed. Brett McKay. N.p., n.d. Web. 14 June 2011. http://artofmanliness.com/about-2

of manhood." He elaborated, noting that while there were cross-cultural similarities, "Being good at being a man for the Kalahari bushman means being able to be persistent and hunt successfully. Being good at being a man for a man living in suburban Ohio probably means holding a job down to support a family, being able to fix things around the house, or if he's single, being adept at interacting with women." McKay told me he thought being a good man was simpler.

He wrote: "developing virtues like honesty, resilience, courage, compassion, discipline, justice, temperance, etc. A man can be a very virtuous and upright man, but be horrible at "being good at being a man." Maybe he can't hunt or he's terrible around women or can't use a hammer to save his life. It's also possible to have a man who's good at being a man, but isn't a good man. You can be the best hunter or mechanic in the world, but if you lie, cheat, steal, you're not a good man." [5]

McKay seemed to say that being good at being a man is like fulfilling a job description, defined by what your culture needs (or wants) men to do, and being a good man has more to do with the kind of moral virtues that Newell advocated. A man can fail at the job of being a man, but still be a good person. I use person here, because these moral values are fairly gender neutral. Perhaps, along these lines of thinking, being a good man is a matter of balancing the cultural demands of manhood with a private commitment to moral uprightness.

McKay's positive prescription for manliness is a welcome change from mainstream "men's magazines," which are more interested in creating sociopathic metrosexual super-consumers than writing positively about manhood. I'd agree with McKay that being good at being a man is rather like a job description, and that the description changes a great deal from culture to culture.

------

5   McKay, Brett. Message to the author. 30 June 2011. E-mail.

However, stopping there plays into the hands of those who say that being a man can mean anything anyone wants it to mean. Is manliness so flexible a concept that a community can re-write the job description however they wish? Not if we accept any model of human nature that acknowledges differences between male and female psychology. Over the past few decades, Americans have transitioned to a service economy and educators treated boys like naughty girls with attitude problems. Males have become less interested in educational achievement, less engaged in political life, less concerned about careers, and more interested in forms of entertainment that feature vicarious gang drama—like video games and spectator sports.[6]

Further, if the "job description" of being a man is written in such a way that the qualities which make a good man are basically identical to the qualities that make a good woman, then those qualities are more about being a good person than anything else. It is good to be honest, just, and kind, but these virtues don't have much specifically to do with being a man. Manliness can't merely be synonymous with "good behavior."

I was raised by a decent family in rural Pennsylvania. I went to Sunday school. I was taught to be polite and respectful to others. I over-tip even when I get crappy service in restaurants, I hold doors for little old ladies, and I'm honest to a fault. When I treat people poorly, I feel bad about it—unless they really had it coming. Like many men, I rebelled against my parent's values when I was younger. However, perhaps like Brett McKay or Tom Matlack, when I later began thinking seriously about masculinity and what it meant, the following phrase kept popping into my head: "I can't think of anything better to be than a good man."

---

6   For more on this, read my short book *No Man's Land*, available online at:

http://www.jack-donovan.com/axis/no-mans-land/

I still can't. My first attempts to describe the value of traditional masculinity in print were laced with the kind of homespun morality I grew up with.

I respect men who try their damnedest to be good men—even when I don't agree with them concerning every little detail about what that means. A lot of men choose careers in law enforcement, firefighting, teaching, or even the military because they truly want to be good men. Wars, laws, and policies aren't always just, but I have to tip my hat to the men who rescue civilians and pull kids out of burning buildings. Only broken hysterics refer to all soldiers and cops as "cannon fodder" or "pigs" or "tools."

However, unless self-sacrifice and restraint are to be masculinity's defining qualities—unless masculinity is to be an ascetic discipline and nothing more—there is a point somewhere down a road of diminishing returns that being a good man is no longer a good trade. There's a point where a man who wants to "feel useful" ends up "feeling used." When the system no longer offers men what they want, how long can you expect them to perform tricks for a pat on the head? How long until the neglected, starving dog turns on its master?

I agree with Newell that there is a long, proud tradition of moral masculinity in the West, and from what I can gather, there are comparable traditions in the East. Muslim men pray five times a day because they, too, want to be good men in their own way.

However, Newell's pitch itself contains a built-in duality: honor *tempered* by prudence, ambition *tempered* by compassion for the suffering and the oppressed, love *restrained* by delicacy—and so forth. Civilized religious and secular attempts to show men how to be good men all seem to include these kinds of checks and balances. These "good man" codes tell men to be manly—but not *too manly*. They advocate restraint. Restraint of what? It seems as though in one hand we have morality and in the other we have something else—a kind of maleness that must be guarded against.

If we allow the moralizers of masculinity to define masculinity for us, we either give ourselves over to the "one true code of masculinity" and become completely ethnocentric about it—which would be the historical norm—or we end up with an endless number of "masculinities," get bogged down in the details of their myriad contradictions and declare, as one famous transgendered sociologist has, "that masculinity is not a coherent object about which a generalizing science can be produced."[7] It is true that if a word or concept can mean anything, it means nothing. Raewyn "Bob" Connell wrote that "claims about a universal basis of masculinity tell us more about the ethos of the claimant than anything else."[8] Connell was a feminist pacifist who advocated the de-gendering of society, as well as a man who wanted to be a woman. He eventually de-gendered himself. His claims about the non-existence of a universal basis of masculinity also revealed *his* own ethos.

All men and women have emotional and material interests when it comes to how masculinity is constructed or deconstructed. True objectivity on this subject is a more or less successful pose. We all have a horse in the race.

For whatever it is worth, scientific evidence for biological *differences* between the sexes and cross-cultural *commonalities* between men has continued to build since Connell published *Masculinities* in 1995, and it is not difficult to find repeated themes in the "hegemonic masculinities" of cultures across the world and throughout history. It is far more difficult to find "masculinities" that have nothing in common. Technolo-

---

7   Connell, Robert William. *Masculinities*. University of California Press, 1995. 67-86. Print.

8   Ibid. 69.

gies and customs vary, but the similarities between cultural ideas of manhood offer more in the way of explaining what it means to be good at being a man than the ephemeral differences. What they have in common has more to do with the gang—with hunting and fighting, with drawing and defending the boundary between *us* and *them*—than it has to do with any culturally specific moral or ethical system.

It's dishonest to pretend that men who don't meet a given set of moral standards are unmanly men. Men may say that immoral men are not real men, but their behavior—including the public admiration for the virility of roguish and criminal types—shows that they don't quite believe this.

To truly understand The Way of Men, we must look for where the masculinity of the gangster overlaps with the masculinity of the chivalrous knight, where modern ideas overlap with ancient ones. We must look at the phenomenon of masculinity *amorally* and as dispassionately as we can. We must find what Man knows for certain, concerning his vital relations to this mysterious Universe. The "religion" of Man is not a moral code, though a man may follow his own code to his death. A man struggles to maintain his honor—his reputation as a man—because some part of him is struggling to earn and maintain a position of value, his status and his sense of belonging within the primal gang. Men want to be good men because good men are well regarded, but being a good man isn't the same as being good at being a man.

There is a difference between being a good man and being good at being a man.

Being a good man has to do with ideas about morality, ethics, religion, and behaving productively within a given civilizational structure. Being a good man may or may not have anything at all to do with the natural role of men in a survival scenario. It is possible to be a good man without being particularly good at being a man. This is an area where men who were good at being men have sought counsel from priests, philosophers, shamans, writers, and historians. The productive synergy between these kinds of men is sadly lost when men of words and ideas pit themselves against men of action, or vice versa. Men of ideas and men of action have much to learn from each other, and the truly great are men of both action and abstraction.

Being good at being a man is about being willing and able to fulfill the natural role of men in a survival scenario. Being good at being a man is about showing other men that you are the kind of guy they'd want on their team if the shit hits the fan. Being good at being a man isn't a quest for moral perfection, it's about fighting to survive. Good men admire or respect bad men when they demonstrate strength, courage, mastery or a commitment to the men of their own renegade tribes. A concern with being good at being a man is what good guys and bad guys have in common.

☠   ☠   ☠

Given enough time, every gang will create some sort of moral code or system of rules to govern its members. Men want to believe they are in the right, and they distinguish themselves by cobbling together some idea of what it means to be right.

In early *mafia* culture, honour meant loyalty "more important than blood ties." Mobsters swore not to make money from prostitution or sleep with each other's wives.[9] They were expected to be family men and were discouraged from wom-

---

9   Dickie, John. *Cosa Nostra : A History of the Sicilian Mafia*. 2004. 31. Palgrave McMillan, 2005. Print.

anizing. If the quote "A man who doesn't spend time with his family can never be a real man," seemed familiar, that's because it was from *The Godfather*.

Yakuza gangs modeled themselves after samurai, and increased their social standing within the larger community by showing generosity and compassion toward the weak and disadvantaged.[10]

One Mexican gang, known as *La Familia Michoacana* recently preached "family values," passed out their own version of the Bible and used some of their profits to help the poor.[11] The leaders of *La Familia* are known to have been influenced by the "macho Christian writing of contemporary American author John Eldredge."[12]

In dire times, men who are not good at being men won't last long enough to worry about being good men. Strength makes all other values possible. As Han said in *Enter the Dragon:* "Who knows what delicate wonders have died out of the world, for want of the strength to survive?"

Men who have accomplished the first job of being men — men who have made survival possible — can and do often concern themselves with being good men. As the bloody boundary between threat and safety moves outward, men have the time and the luxury to cultivate civilized, "higher" virtues.

Gangs of men with separate identities and interests of their own are always a threat to established interests. To pro-

---

10   Kaplan, David E., and Alec Dubro. *Yakuza : Japan's Criminal Underworld*. University of California Press, 2003. 17. Print.

11   Isikoff, Michael. "Feds Crack Down on 'Robin Hood' Drug Cartel." *The Daily Beast (Newsweek)*. N.p., 22 Oct. 2009. Web. 4 Oct. 2011. http://www.thedailybeast.com/newsweek/blogs/declassified/2009/10/22/feds-crack-down-on-robin-hood-drug-cartel.html

12   Gibbs, Stephen. "'Family values' of Mexico drug gang." *BBC News*. BBC, 22 Oct. 2009. Web. 4 Oct. 2011. http://news.bbc.co.uk/2/hi/8319924.stm

tect the interests of those who run our civilized, highly regu-
lated world, men and women are mixed to discourage gang
formation. Feminists, pacifists, and members of the privileged
classes recognize that brother-bonded men who are good at
being men will always be a threat, but forget that some of
those men are necessary to create and maintain order in the
first place. There is a call to do away with what even the United Nations has deemed "outmoded stereotypes" of masculinity that are associated with violence.[13] "Outmoded" is a word
you'll see frequently in academic writing about masculinity.
So-called experts talk about manhood like it was last year's
fad, in part because they subscribe to convenient but discred-
ited blank slate theories about gender being "as lightly linked
to sex as are the clothing, the manners, and the form of head-
dress that a society at a given period assigns to either sex."[14]

Both men and women have attempted to refashion men
to suit their dream of a perfect world. No matter what creed
they profess, whether they want to make "Democratic Men"
or "Fierce Gentlemen" or "Inner Warriors," they can't seem
to escape the gravitational pull of some basic ideas about the
underlying *religion* of men.[15] To appeal to men, they speak
of strength and courage. The moralizers and reimaginers of
masculinity play on a man's primal concern with his status
within the male group, concern for his reputation, his distaste
for being seen as weak, fearful, or inept—they appeal to his
sense of *honor*. Their moralized and reimagined interpreta-

---

13   "Message of the Secretary-General for 2011." *International Day for
the Elimination of Violence against Women 25 November.* Ed. Ban Ki-moon. The
United Nations, 25 Nov. 2011. Web. 9 Jan. 2012.

http://www.un.org/en/events/endviolenceday/sgmessages.shtml

14   Margaret, Mead. *Sex and Temperament: In Three Primitive Societies.*
1935. Harper Perennial, 2001. 262. Print.

15   For more on "Reimagining Masculinity," see *No Man's Land,* available online at:

http://www.jack-donovan.com/axis/no-mans-land/

tions of strength and courage are simply tamed and pacified versions of the old gang virtues, suited to civilized life in a time of peace, plenty, and the sharing of political and economic power with women.

To protect and serve their own interests, the wealthy and privileged have used feminists and pacifists to promote a masculinity that has nothing to do with being good at being a man, and everything to do with being what they consider a "good man." Their version of a good man is isolated from his peers, emotional, effectively impotent, easy to manage, and tactically inept.

A man who is more concerned with being a good man than being good at being a man makes a very well-behaved slave.

There has always been a push and pull between civilized virtues and tactical gang virtues. However, the kind of masculinity acceptable to civilized societies is in many cases related to survival band masculinity. Civilized masculinity requires male gang dramas to become increasingly controlled, vicarious, and metaphorical. Human societies start with the gang, and then grow into nations with sports and a climate of political, artistic, and ideological competition. Eventually—as we see today—average men end up with economic competition and a handful of masturbatory outlets for their caged manhood. When a civilization fails, gangs of young men are there to scavenge its ruins, mark new perimeters, and restart the world.

Remove justice, and what are kingdoms but gangs of criminals on a large scale? What are criminal gangs but petty kingdoms? A gang is a group of men under command of a leader, bound by a compact of association, in which the plunder is divided according to an agreed convention.

If this villainy wins so many recruits from the ranks of the demoralized that it acquires territory, establishes a base, captures cities and subdues people, it then openly arrogates itself the title of kingdom, which is conferred on it in the eyes of the world, not by the renouncing of aggression but by the attainment of impunity.

—St. Augustine, *City of God.* 4-4.

THUG LIFE
The Story of Rome

AS THE STORY GOES, Rome was founded by a gang.

The Romans believed that Romulus and Remus were the distant descendants of Aeneas, who wandered the Mediterranean with a small band of survivors after the ruin of Troy. These exiled Trojans—the few remaining ambassadors of a proud but defeated tradition—were guided by the gods to Latium, where they intermingled with the Latin people of Italy. The former Trojans thrived there, and founded the settlement of Alba Longa—just southeast of modern Rome.

Many generations passed, and the eldest son of each king took the throne until Amulius ousted his older brother Numitor. Amulius murdered Numitor's sons and forced his daughter Rhea Silvia to become a Vestal Virgin, assuring that the exiled Numitor would have no heirs to challenge his own. However, Rhea gave birth to twin boys, and rather than admit an indiscretion, she claimed that they were fathered by Mars, the god of war. King Amulius didn't buy her story. He had her chained and ordered her sons to be drowned in the Tiber river. The men charged with this task left the boys exposed in the swampy shallows of the flooded river and assumed the current would carry them to their deaths. According to legend, it was there that they were rescued by a thirsty she-wolf and suckled on her hairy dugs. The grandsons of Numitor were then discovered by shepherds who took the boys in and raised them as their own.

Thanks in part to a vigorous country life, Romulus and Remus grew into strong young men known for hunting and for fearlessly confronting "wild beasts." They also gained a reputation for attacking robbers, taking their loot and sharing it with all of their shepherd pals. The generous twins were also fun to be around, and their merry band grew.

During a festival, they were ambushed by the bitter robbers and Remus was brought before the King Amulius on poaching charges. While Remus was in custody, Numitor suspected who the twins really were.

Meanwhile, Romulus organized his band of shepherds to kill Amulius and free his brother. The shepherds entered the city separately and gathered together at the last moment to overwhelm Amulius' guard. Romulus succeeded in killing the tyrant king, and after learning his true heritage, he restored the kingship to his grandfather Numitor.

The reunited twins then decided to found a city together on the land where they were raised. However, the two men quarreled over its naming and the dispute became heated. The brothers challenged each other, and in the end Romulus triumphed, killing his beloved twin brother.

Romulus and his friends then set to work organizing the government of the new city that bore his name.

According to the historian Livy, one of the first things that Romulus did after making some rudimentary fortifications was to establish the religious rites that would be celebrated by the people of Rome. In addition to the rites honoring the local gods, Romulus chose to observe the Greek rites of the heroic god-man Hercules, known for his great strength and for his "virtuous deeds." [1]

After identifying a constellation of gods and setting a rough spiritual course for his tribe, Romulus advertised the city of Rome an asylum where all men, freeborn or slave, could start a new life. A motley collection of immigrants from neighboring tribes travelled to Rome, and he selected the best men to help him rule. These men were made *senators* and designated "fathers" (*patres*) of the Roman tribe. Their heirs would be known as patricians. With the city fathers, he created order through law.

Lacking women, the men of Rome knew their city would die with them. Romulus sent out envoys to surrounding communities to secure wives for his men. Their offers of marriage were refused, however, because the young men of Rome had no prospects, no reputations and were generally regarded as a dangerous band of low-born men. Insulted, Romulus and his men hatched a scheme, and invited the people of neighboring communities to a festival. During the festival they seized the unmarried girls. Their parents were furious, and the other tribes affected made war with Rome, but Rome prevailed over all militarily except the Sabines, with whom the women themselves helped to make peace to save both their fathers and their new husbands. The Sabines decided to join the Romans, and it was through this successful "rape" of the Sabine women that Romulus ensured the future of his new tribe.

Romulus continued to strengthen and defend his tribe through calculated military action, and he was loved by the rank and file of his men-at-arms. These rough men—Romulus's big gang—secured the city and made its growth pos-

---

1   Livius, Titus. *The Rise of Rome*. Oxford's World Classics.

sible. They were Rome's guardian class, and their unbeatable fighting spirit would characterize the Roman people for centuries.

One day, as he prepared to review his troops, Romulus disappeared with a violent clap of thunder. Livy suspected that he was torn apart at the hands of his senators, who were contentious and tended to conspire, as men close to power often do. The Roman people preferred to remember Romulus as a great man of divine lineage who lived among the people as one of them, who was known for his meritorious works and courage in battle, and who finally took his rightful place among the gods.

There are many founding myths of cities, and countless myths that establish a totemic lineage of a particular people. In the absence of certain recorded history, this is the myth that Romans chose to believe about themselves. It is the spirit of the tale that endures, and it can tell us something about The Way of Men.

Romulus and Remus were betrayed and abandoned. They were left to die and saved by a wolf. Livy admits that the wolf might have easily been a country whore, but it doesn't really matter—they were raised wild. Romulus and Remus were raised "country." They had practical know-how and they knew the value of a hard day's work. They were given a simple upbringing, uncomplicated by court politics or the soft moral equivocation that attends urban commerce. They were virile and upright youth.

The early life of Romulus and Remus is a Robin Hood story. They roughed up other men, seized their stolen loot and shared it with their poor friends. They were alpha males, natural leaders of men. They were tough, but they weren't bullies. They were the kind of men who other men look up to and want to be around. They were the kind of guys who men choose to lead of their own free will. They had heroic qualities, but they were as flawed as any men—and when the brothers fought for status, as brothers often do, one of them had to lose.

Romulus' "merry men" were basically a gang. They were a rowdy bunch of country boys who came out of nowhere to attack a king and upset the *status quo*. When Romulus staked out his territory and announced that it would be an asylum, he attracted hooligans with little money or status of their own. Some were former slaves. Some could have been wanted men. They had little to lose, everything to gain, and no real investment in the communities they came from. Rome was *Deadwood*; it was The Wild West. Romulus organized these unruly men and established a hierarchy. He founded a culture, a religion, a group identity.

Like any bunch of young men, Romulus' thugs had reproductive interests. Romulus tried the nice route, sending ambassadors out to inquire about getting his men some wives, but his men were laughed out of town. No father of means was going to send his daughter out to some camp to marry a man with no prospects. So Romulus *took* the women. The Romans were able to keep the women and start families because they were strong and effective fighters. They didn't give in. They fought for a new future, and they won.

The Roman tribe used violence and cunning to expand its borders, and men from many tribes became Romans. The expansion of Rome served the interests of the descendants of the tribal fathers: the patrician class. However, Roman economic and military power also benefitted many other citizens and non-citizens living within Roman territory. Protected by Roman might, men were able to specialize and live their lives as laborers, craftsmen, farmer and traders. Many men were able to live relatively non-violent lives. The Roman definition of manliness expanded to include ethical virtues that were less specifically male, but more harmonious with a more complex civilization.

However, the Romans who rested in the lap of protection still hungered for the drama of violence. They became spectators of violence and bloodsport. Gladiators fought each other to the death to entertain the Roman tribe, and the people crowded into massive stadiums like the Circus Maximus to watch chariot races highlighted by gory wrecks. There were chariot racing "color" gangs who brawled after the events like today's soccer hooligans. Political figures, landowners and merchants employed gangs of armed young men to intimidate their opponents, tenants, and business rivals.

Rome was founded by a gang, and it behaved like a gang. To paraphrase St. Augustine, it acquired territory, established a base, captured cities, and subdued people. Then it openly arrogated itself the title of Empire, which was conferred on it in the eyes of the world, not by the renouncing of aggression but by the attainment of (temporary) impunity. Rome slowly collapsed from the inside as it became a giant, pointless, corrupt economic machine. The Roman machine, like the American economic machine, could no longer embody the virile ethos of the small bands of rebellious men responsible for its creation. Gangs of armed young men existed throughout its rise and fall, and there were gangs long after the glory of Rome was left in ruin.

The story of Rome is the story of men and civilization. It shows men who have no better prospects gathering together, establishing hierarchies, staking out land and using strength to assert their collective will over nature, women, and other men.

A CHECK TO CIVILIZATION

What are men supposed to do when there's no land to settle and no one to fight?

One of the basic ideas of evolutionary psychology is that because human evolution occurred over a very long period of time, and then an explosion of technology thrust us into the modern world in a comparatively short period of time (recorded history), humans are more adapted physically and psychologically to the world as it *was* than they are to the world as it *is* today.

Our minds and bodies are adapted to function in a harder world. The situations that make us happy, depressed or afraid have some sort of relationship to our ability to function in what some call the Environment of Evolutionary Adaptedness. The choices we make in the modern world may seem "illogical," but they reflect the kinds of choices we would have made to survive thousands of years ago. Think of all the time, energy and resources we spend on sex even when we have no intention of reproducing. Logic's got nothing to do with it.

Our primal bodies and minds still make their calculations based on the old data. Maybe this is a bug or maybe it's a feature—just in case shit goes down.

The first job of men has always been to keep the perimeter, to face danger, to hunt and fight. Men gather in bands and form a strong group identity. Men run through this pattern over and over again, whether it's logical or not.

Drawing on their understanding of primates, evolutionary biologists Richard Wrangham and Dale Peterson came up with a theory about male gang behavior they dubbed, perhaps unflatteringly, *male demonism.*

> "Demonic males gather in small, self-perpetuating, self aggrandizing bands. They sight or invent an enemy "over there" —across the ridge, on the other side of the boundary, on the other side of a linguistic or social or political or ethnic or racial divide. The nature of the divide hardly seems to matter. What matters is the opportunity to engage in the vast and compelling drama of belonging to the gang, identifying the enemy, going on the patrol, participating in the attack."[1]

Calling this phenomenon "demonism" puts an immoral spin our species' basic survival strategy. It's a strategy that worked for us for a very long time, and a strategy that we'd snap back to in an emergency.

But, once you've founded Rome...what then?

Sometimes there is a good reason to make war, to identify *them* and mobilize *our men* against *theirs*. Sometimes there isn't. Every generation of young men can't be guaranteed a great crisis or war simply to give them an opportunity to explore their "demonic" primal nature or give their lives a sense

---

1   Wrangham, Richard, and Dale Peterson. *Demonic Males : Apes and the Origins of Human Violence.* New York: Mariner Books/Houghton Mifflin Company, 1996. 248. Print.

of meaning. Starting wars for the sake of narrative seems frivolous, though I wonder if we do it subconsciously...out of sheer boredom. Sometimes men pick fights just for something to do—just to *feel* something like the threat of harm and the possibility of triumph.

Most of the time, men seek out substitutes for fighting. In tribal societies, this was probably easy enough. Hunting is something like fighting, and that's why men still do it even though they don't have to. Play fighting—sparring—is part of learning to fight, and men ritualize play fighting with sport.

In 1906 William James called for a "moral equivalent of war." Putting aside the question of whether war is moral or immoral, the phrase "moral equivalent of war" captures our need to suppress and redirect primal masculinity in peacetime. James acknowledged that men seemed to be perpetually in want of some "campaigning" way of life. As a pacifist, he suggested that all young men be drafted for a certain period in a "war against nature" where they could toil and suffer together as fishermen, coal miners, road-builders and so forth.

The idea of a war on nature wouldn't play very well today, but if it were tweaked a bit, it might be the most honest and realistic way to reimagine masculinity. James laughed at the now-vindicated fears of his contemporaries who believed that without a sufficiently warlike nationalism, the United States would degenerate into a society, "of clerks and teachers, of co-education and zo-ophily, of consumer's leagues and associated charities, of industrialism unlimited, and feminism unabashed." However, he also warned that "a permanently successful peace-economy cannot be a simple pleasure-economy."[2]

---

2   James, William. "The Moral Equivalent of War." *Wikisource*. Originally published 1906. Web. 15 Sept. 2011. http://en.wikisource.org/wiki/The_Moral_Equivalent_of_War

William James' plan for peace might have worked for a while, though I doubt any plan for peace is viable in the long term. The problem with outlawing violence is that doing so requires violence, and the problem with outlawing war is that doing so requires universal simultaneous agreement to outlaw war—otherwise the peaceful doves end up sitting ducks.

Whether it would have worked or not, men were never shipped off to fight a war against nature—but we still keep ourselves engaged with "equivalents" of war. Like energy, gang masculinity isn't created or destroyed. This "demonism" is part of what men are and what they've evolved to do. It's always there; it just takes on different forms.

If a civilization is to grow and prosper, the tendency of men to break into gangs becomes an internal security threat. Gangs of men always pose a threat to established interests. "Equivalents" of gang masculinity have the potential to keep men invested in a given society, and to keep them from tearing it apart. Viable substitutes for the masculine "campaigning way of life" keep men from asserting *their own* interests over the interests of the whole, or of those in power.

When men are materially invested in a society—when they believe there is more of what they want to gain by working for the group than by working against it—men will control and redirect their energies in the service of a prosperous society.

When men are emotionally invested in a society—when they feel a strong connection to the group, a strong sense of *us*—men will control and redirect their energies in the service of a peaceful society as long as the most aggressive men (the men who are better at being men) are provided with desirable "equivalents" to gang aggression.

As prosperity and security increase, and the need for men to hunt, struggle and fight decreases, the male desire to engage in gang activity can be controlled and channeled though simulation, vicariousness, and intellectualization.

Simulated Masculinity

- Primal gang aggression and gang bonding are directly simulated through participation in military service, police service, and similar "guardian" activities.

- Primal gang aggression and gang bonding are experienced through participation in ritualized and symbolic gang activities like team sports or cooperative gaming.

- Primal aggression, competitiveness and the need to prove masculinity to the group are channeled through participation in individual sports, survival games, or individual competitions that require demonstrations of strength, courage, or mastery.

Vicarious Masculinity

- Males watch other males participate in wars, guardian work, and survival games.

- Males watch other males participate in team or individual sports.

- Males watch other males demonstrate strength, courage, mastery, or honor.

- Males study the history of males who participated in wars, guardian work, survival games, who participated in team or individual sports, or who have demonstrated strength, courage, mastery, or honor.

- Males read literature and stories about males who participate in wars, guardian work, and survival games, who participate in team or individual sports, or who have demonstrated strength, courage, mastery, or honor.

- Males watch films or plays about males who participate in wars, guardian work, and survival games, who participate in team or individual sports, or who have demonstrated strength, courage, mastery, or honor.

Intellectualized Masculinity

- **Economic aggression and gang activity** – men or groups of men compete to outwit each other through economic competition. They demonstrate strength and courage by testing each other to see who is going to back down first and who is going to press his interests furthest. One example is a commissioned salesman selling an automobile to an informed buyer. Economic masculinity is demonstrated by taking risks and believing that you are competent enough to prevail. Companies benefit from intellectualized masculinity when men are more productive because they are encouraged to compete against each other.

- **Political/ideological aggression and gang activity** – men form political or ideological teams and compete to win debates and battles of wit and strategy. Examples include political strategy, philosophical debate, academic or scientific debate, religious debate and the guys who spend hours on message boards and comment threads trying to prove they are right about almost anything.

- **Metaphorical masculinity** – for religious, ideological, or personal reasons, men turn masculinity inward. External battles become metaphors for internal battles, and the focus is on self-mastery, impulse control, disciplined behavior and perseverance. Men struggle to be good men, to be rational men, to be good fathers, to be good citizens, to be faithful men, to invent and create, to achieve goals.

- **Ascetic masculinity** – the self-mastery and self-discipline of metaphorical masculinity lead to a tunneled focus on self-denial and the rejection of natural male desires for sex, food, worldly things, virile action, or violence.

I first envisioned simulated, vicarious, and intellectual masculinity as a progression running in one direction. My thinking was that as societies become safer and more prosperous, masculinity is simulated, then mostly vicarious, then mostly intellectualized. That makes some sense in the very big picture, but it doesn't work exactly like that.

Most or all of these substitutes for gang masculinity have been present in every kind of social organization and civilization. There have almost always been sports, and men who enjoyed watching sports and other contests of strength, speed, or agility. Primitive and civilized peoples alike have told stories of great deeds and reflected on what it meant to be a good man. Humans have been trading and negotiating for a long time, and there have almost always been priests and monks and ascetics.

Further, most or all of these methods of channeling gang masculinity can be present in and important to any given man. There are and have always been pious warriors and athletes. Manly men are generally expected to be good men, to exercise self-restraint, and to behave ethically. Men who we see as men of action will still take political sides or debate with one another. Men who play sports usually enjoy watching them. Overcoming internal struggles is essential to overcoming external struggles, to surviving, and to achieving anything.

So, both individual men and civilizations can and do channel masculinity through simulation, vicariousness, *and* intellectualization at any point in their development. What changes is emphasis and opportunity.

Because gangs are a threat to order unless they are organized in the service of a civilization, opportunities for the direct experience of gang masculinity—participation in warmaking, protecting and defending—will generally be available to a smaller proportion of the male population as the big gang that runs the civilization through one means or another "attains impunity." Some men will fight, but fewer. Modern technology speeds this up. If you have the ability to attack safely and *indirectly* with remote drones, few men will ever have to kill anyone *directly*.

The plenty produced by modern technology also reduces the opportunity for men to engage in "wars on nature," as James put it. Fewer and fewer men will be required to work actively with their hands as they would have in a primitive survival gang. Agriculture will replace group hunting, and machine-driven agribusiness or state-run agriculture will turn the trade of farming into a low-skill "job" that requires no emotional investment from men. Hunting gives way to the conveyor-belt slaughterhouse, and the efficiency of that system ensures that even fewer men will be required to participate in the hunting process. Hunting survives for most men only as a sport. We get our meat from the supermarket. For most of us today, what we do to get the money to buy the meat has little or nothing to do with hunting. It doesn't have to happen this way, but it has.

As *opportunities* for men to do what they evolved to do decrease, greater *emphasis* is placed on simulated, vicarious, and intellectualized channels of masculinity to maintain order and cultural unity. Men still get to *feel* like men, but the threat that men pose to order, to established interests, and to the interests of women is mitigated.

Men compete for status and they want to earn peer approval, so the channels for masculinity that appeal to them will be related to their natural aptitudes and temperament. Guys with thin frames and high metabolisms may not make the best powerlifters, but they usually make good runners. Likewise, intellectuals and verbally gifted men take especially well to intellectualized channels of masculinity.

Most men are talented evenly enough that they can remain engaged by a mix of simulated, intellectualized and vicarious forms of masculinity so long as they are otherwise invested in a given civilization.

A minority of men need extremely frequent opportunities for vital, immediate equivalents to hunting and war as they can get to keep them productive, and to keep them from self-destructing. Charles Darwin thought that these "restless" men were a "great check to civilization," but that they could "make useful pioneers."[3] These men tend to get into a lot of trouble in higher civilizations—they fill our prisons and often have problems with substance abuse—whereas they'd probably do pretty well in a survival scenario.

Another small number of men are happy to live almost completely in their heads, and are easily satisfied by intellectual pursuits and abstract demonstrations of masculinity. Just as jocks brag that real men play sports because they are good at them, abstract thinkers will pretend they have conquered their baser instincts by simply doing what *they* are naturally good at. Men compete for status, and they want to feel like they are winning.

Once you recognize this, debates between men about the true nature of masculinity become amusingly predictable. Engineers think manhood is all about technology, liberal arts majors think it is about civilized virtue, and athletes think masculinity is all about strength, speed and perseverance. Effeminate males think they are more "evolved" than their brutish brothers, and thus, the truly better men. In a balanced, unified, patriarchal society that provides opportunities for the majority of men to put their talents to use, all of those guys can be right—at least partially. They can all demonstrate strength, courage, mastery and honor to their peers in different ways, and they can all feel valued by a set of peers. Ideally, those guys could cultivate a modicum of respect for their different roles—though since status seeking is the way of men, men with healthy egos will usually believe that their own role is just a little more important, and a little bit better.

Unfortunately, we've reached a level of civilization, technology and plenty that—to protect order and established interests—opportunities for vital, immediate equivalents to hunting and war are increasingly rare. Weapons technology has made war too deadly and too easy for men willing to

---

3   Darwin, Charles. *The Descent of Man.* Orig. 1871. New Century Books. Kindle. Loc. 2623-2624.

use that technology to get what they want at all costs. Lawyers and insurance companies—and more technology—have made dangerous, exciting and engaging jobs safe, easy and boring. Only a select few guardians, workers in shrinking and outsourced fields and men who favor intellectual channels of masculinity are satisfactorily engaged in activities where they feel like they are risking, struggling, and winning. Everyone else is just playing around, and they know it. Men are dropping out and disengaging from our slick, easy, safe world. For what may be the first time in history, the average guy can afford to be careless. Nothing he does really matters, and—what's worse—there is a shrinking hope of any future where what he does *will* matter.

Pornography is not the same as sex. It's a substitute for it. Would pornography lose its appeal without the possibility of sex? Will war and survival simulations be enough without even the remotest possibility of war or strife? Will they simply become empty, depleting, and depressing?

This is one reason why people love zombie movies and "disaster porn" so much. The apocalypse—any apocalypse—offers an opportunity. As the back cover of *The Walking Dead* comic book reads, "In a world ruled by the dead, we are forced to finally start living."

The compromise between modern civilization and manliness promoted by intellectuals is, predictably, an increased emphasis on intellectualized channels for masculinity. There are a few problems with this.

For starters, not all men are intellectuals, so they are going to suck at that game. No one likes losing all the time—ask any nerd or fag who has been bullied. If only a minority of men are intellectuals, and intellectualized masculinity is all we have, the majority of men are going to feel like they are losing all the time. If you want to create a society of listless antisocial losers, convince the majority of your men that they're already losing, and that no matter what they do, they will never be able to win.

What's the point in trying if you know the game is rigged?

For the satisfaction of knowing you are contributing to the greater good?

That's just the kind of stupid thing an intellectual would say.

Another problem with the complete intellectualization of masculinity is that intellectualized masculinity is pretty much equally accessible to women. Demonstrating your manliness to other men doesn't mean much if women are doing all of the same things that men are doing. "Intellectual courage" isn't particularly specific to men or the role of men. Women can be equally "intellectually courageous." Women can screw each other over in business just as well as men can—maybe even better. Women can demonstrate self-mastery, they can be good citizens. Women can be morally upright and while as a group they lag in the sciences, there are women who can compete with men in every academic field. Intellectualized masculinity is only workable when masculinity is intellectualized differently than femininity and men are not forced to compete with women. If men are subconsciously trying to demonstrate their worthiness as men to other men, and then find themselves competing with women, it kind of blows the whole illusion.

The introduction of women into a field of competition short-circuits its viability as a substitute for male gang activity.

Competition doesn't satisfy the same primal need in most men when women are involved—no matter how the women behave, or how rational the reason for including them may seem. As a general rule, if you introduce women into the mix, men either shift their focus from impressing each other to impressing the women, or they lose interest altogether and do just enough to get by.

Feminist demands for absolute equality and the integration of the sexes into war and its equivalents—combined with the looming threat of technological mass destruction and the desire of globalist elites to protect their investments against ornery gangs of men—have pushed the intellectualization of masculinity into a terminal phase: ***repudiation***. Accepting the nature of men as it is and offering them equivalents to war is no longer acceptable to women or globalists. Their shared agenda has become the complete repudiation of the idea that men should want to do the things they've been selected to do.

Boys are scolded even for their violent fantasies—for the violent stories they want to hear, the violent books they want to read, the violent games they want to play. Male "demonism" is punished, pathologized, and stigmatized from cradle to campus. Even the good guys are treated like bad guys for ganging up, for being "xenophobic," patriotic, or too exclusive. Video games, fighting sports, and movies are decried for being "too violent." Football is deemed "too dangerous" by many overprotective parents. Everyone is supposed to agree that violence is never the answer—unless that violence comes from the cutting edge of the State's axe.

Only those natural ascetics and intellectuals will truly be satisfied by the repudiation of gang masculinity as a substitute for gang masculinity. For most men, this repudiation of the role of men and our species' basic survival strategy will feel—rightly—like self hatred and oppression. The Way of Men is to gang up and fight each other, or fight nature. Teaching men to despise that is teaching them to despise their history, to hate their own talents and to reject their natural place in the world.

The repudiation of violent masculinity is the murder of male identity.

It's handicapping them and condemning them to a life of losing by cutting off their best chance at winning. Cultural repudiation of The Way of Men extinguishes the dream of virile action and makes its equivalents seem hollow and base. It erases the secret hope of men—the fantasy that one day they will be tested, that one day they will be thrust into a dire world at the bloody edge between life and death where everything they do will really matter.

In a recent column for *Asia Times*, Spengler argued that cultures facing their own imminent demise implode or lash out. They operate under a different standard of rationality, like a man who has been diagnosed with a terminal illness. Our modern idea of rational behavior fails to comprehend that kind of spiritual crisis. He wrote:

> "Individuals trapped in a dying culture live in a twilight world. They embrace death through infertility, concupiscence, and war. A dog will crawl into a hole to die. The members of sick cultures do not do anything quite so dramatic, but they cease to have children, dull their senses with alcohol and drugs, become despondent, and too frequently do away with themselves. Or they may make war on the perceived source of their humiliation."[4]

The restless men who sense that they will never be pioneers—who will never build the fire, keep watch over the

---

4   Goldman, David P. (aka. "Spengler") "The fifth horseman of the apocalypse." *Asia Times Online* 13 Dec. 2011. Web. 6 Feb. 2012.

http://atimes.com/atimes/Global_Economy/ML13Dj05.html

camp or fight for their lives—may turn out to be the check of civilization. Look at what hopeless, directionless, angry young black men have done to the cities that were never theirs. See how well the once-proud Aztecs reacted to the rape of their cities and foreign rule. White men are equally capable of bringing down a future they have no place in—a future built on dreams that are not their own.

The emotional needs of men are not being met by a world that repudiates The Way of Men, but so long as their material needs are being met, men may choose not to make war against the world. As long as they have enough stuff, enough food, enough distractions—men may be content to dull their senses, tune out, and allow themselves to become slaves to the interests of women, bureaucrats and wealthy men.

THE BONOBO MASTURBATION SOCIETY

What would happen if men got spoiled, gave up and gave in to women completely? How would that society operate?

The evolutionary theory of parental investment suggests that because reproduction is costly, members of the sex which makes the lesser parental investment will compete for sexual access to whichever sex makes the greater parental investment. In humans and most mammals, females are forced to make the greatest investment in reproduction.

Human females carry their children for nine months, and they are highly vulnerable and less mobile during the later stages of pregnancy. Giving birth itself is traumatic, and death during childbirth was more common in the past than it is today. After birth, the mother remains especially vulnerable for a short period. A human child is extremely vulnerable for several months, and will remain vulnerable for several years. Nursing is another investment required of human mothers until recently.

Human males have it comparatively easy. We can pass on our genes in a matter of minutes, and then skip town unless we are persuaded to stick around by females, social controls, or shotgun-wielding fathers.

Human males evolved to compete for access to females because female reproductive investment is a valuable prize. Males can exist in the all-male world of the gang, but females quite literally represent the future. Men create a perimeter and establish security. They create a rudimentary hierarchy, order and seminal culture of *us* vs. *them*. To perpetuate the *us*, they need women. So they try to figure out how to get women, and how to get "access to their reproductive investment."

Major West, a character in the zombie movie *28 Days Later*, tells a story reminiscent of the founding of Rome. He gives the rationale for the rape of the Sabine women in just a few lines:

> "Eight days ago, I found Jones with his gun in his mouth. He said he was going to kill himself because there was no future. What could I say to him? We fight off the infected or we wait until they starve to death... and then what? What do nine men do except wait to die themselves? I moved us from the blockade, and I set the radio broadcasting, and I promised them women. Because women mean a future."[1]

The Way of Men is the Way of The Gang, but a gang of men, alone, has no future. The all-male gang ends with the death of the last man. Men want to be remembered, they want their tradition to survive, and they want sex. Ultimately, these psychological mechanisms and desires will allow them to pass on their genes. When there is competition for resources—including women—it is good strategy for a gang of men to create a patriarchal hierarchy, eliminate neighboring rival

---

1   *28 Days Later*. Writ. Alex Garland. 2002. 20th Century Fox. DVD-ROM.

gangs, take their women, and protect the women from rival gangs. This is exactly what many primitive tribes do. This is the basic strategy of the gang.

What happens when competition for resources is radically reduced?

What happens when women get *their* way?

Two of our closest primate relatives, chimpanzees and bonobos, illustrate some of the differences between the way of males and the way of females.

Wrangham and Peterson argued that in spite of cultural determinist theories and a lot of wishful thinking about peaceful pre-historic matriarchies—the evolutionary, archaeological, historical, anthropological, physiological and genetic evidence overwhelmingly suggests that humans have always been a patriarchal, male-bonded party-gang species that engaged in regular coalitionary violence. This was a brave conclusion, because both authors seemed to be wholeheartedly against violence. As self-described evolutionary feminists, they offered suggestions as to how we might end male violence now that men have the means to wreak havoc well beyond what their primitive ancestors could do with powerful arms and simple tools. Aside from selective breeding to reduce violent alpha tendencies in males—a program that seems to be underway, albeit accidentally—and the establishment of one world government, Wrangham and Peterson suggested that we look to the gentle bonobo apes for guidance.

Chimpanzees and bonobos are both close relatives of humans. Both have much in common with people, but when it comes to social structures, the chimps are more apt to live in small groups led by a hierarchical gang of males, whereas the bonobos tend to live in larger, more stable parties with a greater number of females and the females maintain coalitions that check male violence. Chimpanzees organize to the benefit of male reproductive interests, and bonobos organize to the benefit of female reproductive interests. Chimps follow The Way of Men. Bonobos follow The Way of Women.

THE CHIMPANZEE WAY

Chimpanzees can mingle in larger parties if they are able to make alliances, and if food is plentiful. Chimps and humans prefer high-quality foods, and male chimps actively hunt for meat, especially red colobus monkeys. Chimpanzees compete for resources when they are scarce, so they break up into smaller gangs. This is a "party-gang" social structure because of this flexibility in party size. Under stress, they revert to patriarchal gangs run by male relatives and bonded male allies. Females move (and are moved) from gang to gang. Males compete for sexual access to females, but males also sometimes court the females and escort them away from the stress of male competition. Females who do not have children sometimes join males in hunting and raiding activities. Females are subordinate to males in the chimpanzee social hierarchy, and they are expected to demonstrate submission. When a young male comes of age, he will usually make a big show of it, and start pushing females around until they acknowledge him as an adult male. After he achieves that, he'll stop making such a big to do. However, chimpanzee males do batter females sporadically to maintain their status and show the gals what's what. Males who come of age spend a lot of time together, but also spend a lot of time competing for status with each other. Their contests are often violent, and on rare occasions two males have been known to form an alliance and murder the alpha male. Humans might recognize this as patricide or tyrannicide. For chimps, in-group competition is less important than competition with other groups. Chimpanzees and humans are the only two members of the great apes where males form coalitions to go out and raid or eliminate members of a neighboring gang. Alpha chimps will occasionally gather up other males, go out to the edge of their range, try to catch a member of another gang unaware, and murder him. This is similar to the "skulking way of war" common among primitive humans, who also engage in guerilla raiding[2]. Over time, males will pick off all of the other males of the neighbor gang, absorb the remaining females into their own group, and mate with them. Because chimpanzees hunt, defend and aggress as a coordinated gang, they have to be willing to put aside internecine competition and maintain close bonds with each other. Primatologist Frans de Waal wrote:

> "...the chimpanzee male psyche, shaped by millions of years of intergroup warfare in the natural habitat, is one of both competition and compromise. Whatever the level of competition among them, males count on each other against the outside. No male ever knows when he will need his greatest foe. It is, of course, this mixture of camaraderie and rivalry among males that makes chimpanzee society so much more recognizable to us than the social structure of the other great apes."[3]

THE BONOBO WAY

Bonobos eat many of the same foods that chimpanzees like, and they will eat meat when they find it. However, bonobos don't share their territory with gorillas, so they are able to eat the kinds of portable herbs that gorillas eat. Wrang-

---

2   Keeley, Lawrence H. *War Before Civilization*. Oxford University Press, 1996. 1,016-172. Kindle.

3   de Waal, Frans. *Chimpanzee Politics*. 1982. Baltimore: Johns Hopkins Paperbacks, 2000. 1,055-58. Kindle.

ham and Peterson believe that this is one of the key differences between chimps and bonobos. Bonobos have a staple food source that is easy to find. They don't have to compete for resources even when many foods are out of season, so they can more or less relax all year long in a peace of plenty. The males compete for status, but they seem less concerned about it because status for bonobo males doesn't mean much. Bonobos don't compete for mates. Each male just waits his turn, and the females are happy to oblige anyone who comes knocking. For the bonobos sex is social, and bonobos have both homosexual and heterosexual sex. Bonobo males don't know who their kids are, because any of the kids could be their kids. The mother makes all of the parental investment. Bonobo males do know who their mothers are, and they remain bonded to them for life—they often follow their mothers around throughout adulthood, and mothers intervene in conflicts on a behalf of their sons. Males don't spend a lot of time together in bonobo groups, but females build strong friendships with one another. When males start trouble, the females band together to put a stop to it quickly. Bonobo females are in charge. When one group of bonobos comes in contact with another group, the female bonobos will be the ones who make the peace, and generally they will start engaging in *hoka-hoka* with each other—that's what natives call bonobo girl-on-girl action. Then the females will start mating with the males from the opposite group. The males just sit around and watch, shrug their shoulders and eventually join in.

A CONFLICT OF INTERESTS

Bonobos and chimpanzees are adapted to different environments, and their social structures follow from what those environments have to offer. Bonobo society favors female interests. Female coalitions hold sway over politics, and female bonding is more important than male bonding. Males are bonded to their mothers and don't know who their fathers are. Females stay together for life. In chimpanzee society, females are somewhat isolated and stay with their young when they are children, while males enjoy both rivalry and camaraderie, and stay with their fathers, brothers and male friends for life. Chimpanzee society favors male interests.

Wrangham and Peterson believe that bonobos offer a "threefold path to peace" because they have managed to reduce violence between the sexes, reduce violence between males, and reduce violence between communities.[4] In response to the mass destruction inherent to modern warfare, many men have searched for ways to abandon the "warfare system"[5] that attends patriarchy, and they have looked to women for guidance on coalition building and finding a more peaceful way to live.

Those who believe human warfare is somehow unnatural will find little objective support for this theory in history or the sciences. Human societies are complex, and aspects of both bonobo and chimpanzee patterns are familiar enough. But male aggression, male coalitional violence, and male political dominance have all been identified as "human universals"—meaning that evidence of these behaviors have been found in some form in almost every human society that has ever been studied.[6]

Scientists only began to study bonobos as a separate and distinct species in the 1950s, because bonobos evolved

---

4   Wrangham, Richard, and Dale Peterson. 205.

5   Keen, Sam. *Fire in the Belly*. Bantam, 1991. Chapter 8, "A Brief History of Manhood." Print. 1,655-2,110. Kindle.

6   Brown, Donald E. "Human Universals." DePaul University, n.d. Web. 19 Feb. 2011. http://condor.depaul.edu/mfiddler/hyphen/humunivers.htm

in a small, sheltered range. Chimpanzees have a much larger range, and have adapted to more diverse environments. Humans and chimps clearly have more in common in terms of social organization. It is likely that while humans are smarter and have far more complex social arrangements than chimpanzees, male bonding and male coalitional violence have been constant features of human and pre-human societies.

The following table shows the differences between various aspects of chimpanzee societies and bonobo societies—it shows two ways, two extremes.

MALE INTERESTS vs. FEMALE INTERESTS

	Male Interests (Chimpanzees)	Female Interests (Bonobos)
Resources	Variable, sometimes difficult to obtain	Readily available
Hunting Priority	High	Low
Male Alliances	Yes	No
Female Alliances	No	Yes
Sexuality	For mating	For pleasure and socialization
Homosexuality	Minimal, uncommon	Frequent, common
Political Dominance	Males	Shared, but female coalitions have most influence
Males - Parent Bonding	Father, Brothers, patrilineal Males spend time with mothers during youth, with males for the rest of their lives, with females for mating	Mothers, matrilineal, generally stay in party
Males Batter Females	Yes	No
Male Rape Females	Yes, but rare	Why bother?
Females Acknowledge Male Dominance	Yes	No
Range Defended	Yes	Sometimes
Intergroup Raiding	Yes	No
Border Patrols	Yes	No

Some researchers have suggested that bonobos aren't as peaceful as Wrangham and Peterson believed, but it does seem clear that they are more peaceful and matriarchal than chimps, and that their lifestyle is similar to what I've described.

As a metaphor for what happens to men living in a secure peace of plenty like our own, the bonobo way looks eerily familiar.

Aren't most men today spoiled mamma's boys without father figures, without hunting or fighting or brother-bonds, whose only masculine outlet is promiscuous sex?

Wars against men are known to fewer and fewer of us. Mandatory conscription for the Vietnam War ended the year before I was born. Since then, the United States has effectively created a class of professional contract soldiers who do the government's fighting in faraway lands. Average men know more about collegiate basketball than they know about a given overseas conflict.

Like the bonobos, we don't have to worry about hunger. We barely have a reason to get up off the couch. Until the recent extended recession, jobs were fairly easy to come by, and almost all of the men who wanted to work were able to get a job. Welfare and social assistance programs provide safety nets for many others, and few American men living today grew up in a home without a television. True hunger and poverty and desperation, the way people know it in Africa, is rare even for those who are officially considered poor. Diseases that wiped out populations in the past are treatable, and people recover fully from injuries that would have been fatal one hundred years ago. If anything illustrates the surreal plenty we live in today, it is the fact that we have problems like epidemic *obesity*. People are able to sit in their homes and eat until they are so fat they can't move.

Americans are obese in part because they simply don't *do* enough. It's hard to find a job doing the kind of back-breaking work our ancestors did. I know, because I'm the kind of person who thinks a temp job digging ditches sounds like fun. *I've actually looked.* Our bodies have a tremendous capacity for work when we are conditioned for it. The human body is made to work hard. When there is no work to do, our physical health deteriorates. Doctors have to tell people to walk like it is some kind of breakthrough exercise technology. Once, I watched in awe as a personal trainer authoritatively led a pair of forty-something adults on a walk around their own neighborhood. He was a seventy-five dollar an hour human dog-walker.

The rest of us go to the gym to "work out," which is just a substitute for doing physical work. People who answer emails for a living go to a special building where they trick their bodies into thinking they are actually doing the kind of work humans evolved to do. Activities like sandbag training and stone lifting and barefoot running are becoming popular. It's only a matter of time before someone comes up with a way to market a fitness craze where people run around spearing rubber mammoths.

The goal of civilization seems to be to eliminate work and risk, but the world has changed more than we have. Our bodies crave work and sex, our minds crave risk and conflict.

It has always been striking to me that even in our most popular visions of the future, we have been unable to eliminate conflict. Take *Star Trek*, for instance. On the surface, *Star Trek* is a modernist, feminist, egalitarian dream. Men and women and people of all races work side-by-side in a one-world meritocracy that seeks peace across the universe. But our fantasy isn't the peace, it's the conflict. Without some conflict between *us* and *them*, there is no plot. On *Star Trek,* they're always fighting someone. Many are attracted to peaceful platitudes like the ones heard in John Lennon's "Imagine," but people aren't actually very good, or very interested, in imagining a future without conflict. If someone wrote a sci-fi show without conflict, would anyone watch?

We are pretty good, however, at imagining inventive ways to masturbate our primal natures with "safe" virtual, vicarious, and abstract pleasures.

Our society has almost no tolerance for unsanctioned physical violence. Children are expelled from school for fighting, and something as historically common as a weaponless, drunken brawl can land men in court or in jail.

As coalitions of females, pandering politicians and fearful men organize to child-proof our world, to ban guns and regulate violent sports, men retreat to redoubts of virtual and vicarious masculinity like video games and fantasy football because it's all they have left.

People are also seeking out other non-violent forms of simulated risk and "safe" adventure. From skydiving and bungee-jumping to guided mountaineering and adventure races, men and women are coming up with more and more ways to simulate the primitive human experience. Women and men have similar drives in different degrees, and what I've noticed while participating in 5Ks and CrossFit and the "Warrior Dash" is that after the novelty of it wears off, attendance often becomes increasingly female. While some women participate competitively, many more women enjoy these experiences socially and emotionally, stopping along the way to cheer and encourage their struggling sisters. I get the sense that many husbands and boyfriends recognize the masturbatory, "feel-good" nature of these activities and shrug their shoulders, wondering why they would run through the mud in ninety degree heat *for no good reason*. From an evolutionary standpoint, it makes sense that women would tend to prefer and be more satisfied with "safe" and "fun" risk simulation, while men would long for real competition, real risk, and the potential for real status gains. The carefully orchestrated, sanitized, padded, insured and permitted exercise rarely compares to the fantasy of virile action and meaningful risk.

In video games, at least men experience *virtual* death.

As physical competition for resources has decreased, sex has become increasingly social, as it is for the bonobos. Men and women hook up to satisfy their primal drive to reproduce. To the chagrin of masculinity's reimaginers, women still respond sexually to the kinds of "alpha" traits and behaviors in men that would have made them good hunters and fighters. Displaying strength, courage and mastery signals genetic superiority and high male status to women—even women who have no plans to reproduce. Men seek out women who appear to be hearty and fertile, and women trick men's monkey brains with lipstick, liposuction and breast implants. Sex today is increasingly disconnected from mating, and for many it has become a matter of "masturbating with someone else's body."

In many cases, what that body offers is a disappointment compared to the risk-free sex that men can have virtually and vicariously through immediately available, high-quality pornography. In 2003, feminist Naomi Wolf[1] and writer David Amsden[2] wrote that the simulated sexual experience was turning many men off to sex with real women, who felt that they had to compete with pornography for the attention of men.

2003…wasn't that back when people actually still paid for porn, and a gigabyte still sounded like a big file? Today young men can download high definition pornography in moments

---

1   Wolf, Naomi. "The Porn Myth." *New York Magazine.* 20 Oct. 2003. Web. 18 Sept. 2011. http://nymag.com/nymetro/news/trends/n_9437/

2   Amsden, David. "Not Tonight, Honey. I'm Logging On." *New York Magazine.* 20 Oct. 2003. Web. 18 Sept. 2011. http://nymag.com/nymetro/news/trends/n_9349/

and watch it on the same dazzling big screen television that they bought to watch the Super Bowl. *New York Magazine* followed up in 2011 with a story titled, "He's Just Not That Into Anyone" wherein the author reported faking an orgasm during real sex, but having no problems climaxing when watching porn. Some of the men he interviewed for the story told him that they were experiencing erectile dysfunction during real sex, and others told him they had to replay scenes from porn to get off while fucking their wives. Singer John Mayer confessed to *Playboy* magazine that there had probably been days where he had seen three hundred vaginas before getting out of bed.[3]

Our world isn't offering men more paths to virile fulfillment or vital experience.

What the modern world offers average men is a thousand and one ways to safely spank our monkey brains into oblivion.

Is it any wonder that some men ask themselves, in lucid moments between masturbating to various forms of vicarious sex and violence, what Betty Friedan wrote that educated housewives were asking themselves in the fifties:[4]

"Is this all?"

We were born into a peace of plenty, a pleasure-economy, a bonobo masturbation society.

The future that our elite handlers have in store for us advertises more of the same. More detached pleasure, less risk, freedom from want, more masturbation. Reimaginers of masculinity offer us metaphorical battles to fight, but in the real

---

3   Rothbart, Davy. "He's Just Not That Into Anyone." *New York Magazine*. 30 Jan. 2011. Web. 18 Sept. 2011. http://nymag.com/news/features/70976/

4   Friedan, Betty. *The Feminine Mystique*. 1963. Dell Publishing, 1983. 15. Print.

world the most meaningful battles will be "fought" between elite bureaucrats and experts and wealthy managers who believe they know what is best, while the rest of us shuffle off to boring, risk-free jobs to do idiot work and stare at the clock, waiting to go home and furiously indulge ourselves in whatever form of vicarious or virtual primitive experience gets us off.

Cosmopolitan journalists from elite schools like Betty Friedan filled women's imaginations with fantasies of exciting big-city careers that only a few could ever hope to attain. For every woman living that fantasy today, there are a bunch of women scanning merchandise through a checkout line at some big-box retail store, or doing repetitive data-entry in some gray office. In the East, women are answering our phone calls or performing monotonous assembly line tasks in factories. This is called "progress." Many of those women would probably rather be spending more time actively engaged in the lives of their children, but they no longer have the choice to stay home.

The cost of civilization is a progressive trade-off of vital existence. It's a trade of the real for the artificial, for the convincing con, made for the promise of security and a full belly.

It has always been so.

The question is: "how much trade is too much?"

In the future that globalists and feminists have imagined for themselves, only a few people will actually do anything worth doing. A few people will be scientists, charged with uncovering the mysteries of the universe. A few people will be engineers who dream and design and solve problems. A few people will inhabit a privileged managerial class of financiers and bureaucrats, and they will make all of the decisions that matter for everyone else. They will captain companies and departments and build their great Leviathans out of legal papers and fake smiles. There will also be, as there is now, a glamorous creative class charged with devising our sedentary entertainments. There will be gladiators and chariot races. There will be drama and theater people, and there will be global village gossip.

Still, everyone can't be a chief, and most of us will be Indians. Products need hordes of consumers and salespeople and customer service representatives and clerks and stock boys and loss prevention associates and midnight janitors. Anyone on the left hand side of the bell curve, anyone who makes the wrong choices at the wrong time, anyone who doesn't jump through the hoops or play the game, anyone who hasn't been "properly socialized," and anyone who turns down the wrong options for the right reasons will end up doing those drone jobs. As Matthew B. Crawford observed in his book *Shop Class As Soulcraft*, even so-called white-collar "knowledge work" is "subject to routinization and degradation, proceeding by the same logic that hit manufacturing a hundred years ago: the cognitive elements of the job are appropriated from professionals, instantiated in a system or process, and then handed back to a new class of workers—clerks—who replace the professionals."[5] Being able to read and write at a college level doesn't mean the job you do will require much more thinking or consequential problem solving than you would have to do as a shift manager at McDonalds. It will only save you from the greasy forehead.

Only a couple hundred years ago, many of these men now destined for clerkdom would have learned a trade from their fathers and mastered it, whether it was farming or some other kind of engaging work that they could be proud of. They would have been valued members of a smaller community of people who cared whether they lived or died. Some would have spent their lives with gangs of men on ships, but most would have been bound to provide for and protect their

---

5   Matthew, Crawford B. *Shop Class As Soulcraft : an inquiry into the value of work*. Penguin Books, 2010. 44. Print.

families—their own small clans. This was a workable compromise between gang life and family life. A few generations ago, these men would have had meaningful responsibilities and their actions would have had the potential to do more harm than merely hurting someone's feelings or causing them to be inconvenienced. They would have had pressing reasons to try to be good at being men, but also to be good men. Not so long ago, these men would have had dignity and honor.

In the future that globalists and feminists have imagined, for most of us there will only be more clerkdom and masturbation. There will only be more apologizing, more submission, more asking for permission to be men. There will only be more examinations, more certifications, mandatory prerequisites, screening processes, background checks, personality tests, and politicized diagnoses. There will only be more medication. There will be more presenting the secretary with a cup of your own warm urine. There will be mandatory morning stretches and video safety presentations and sign-off sheets for your file. There will be more helmets and goggles and harnesses and bright orange vests with reflective tape. There can only be more counseling and sensitivity training. There will be more administrative hoops to jump through to start your own business and keep it running. There will be more mandatory insurance policies. There will definitely be more taxes. There will probably be more Byzantine sexual harassment laws and corporate policies and more ways for women and protected identity groups to accuse you of misconduct. There will be more micro-managed living, pettier regulations, heavier fines, and harsher penalties. There will be more ways to run afoul of the law and more ways for society to maintain its pleasant illusions by sweeping you under the rug. In 2009 there were almost five times more men either on parole or serving prison terms in the United States than were actively serving in all of the armed forces.[6]

If you're a good boy and you follow the rules, if you learn how to speak passively and inoffensively, if you can convince some other poor sleepwalking sap that you are possessed with an almost unhealthy desire to provide outstanding customer service or increase operational efficiency through the improvement of internal processes and effective organizational communication, if you can say stupid shit like that without laughing, if your record checks out and your pee smells right—you can get yourself a J-O-B. Maybe you can be the guy who administers the test or authorizes the insurance policy. Maybe you can be the guy who helps make some soulless global corporation a little more money. Maybe you can get a pat on the head for coming up with the bright idea to put a bunch of other guys out of work and outsource their boring jobs to guys in some other place who are willing to work longer hours for less money. Whatever you do, no matter what people say, no matter how many team-building activities you attend or how many birthday cards you get from someone's secretary, you will know that you are a completely replaceable unit of labor in the big scheme of things.

No sprawling bureaucracy or global corporation can ever love you. They have public relations budgets and human re-

---

6   Glaze, Lauren. "NCJ 231681 : Correctional Populations In The United States, 2009." Office of Justice Programs. Bureau of Justice Statistics, 21 Dec. 2010. Web. 2 Oct. 2011.

http://bjs.ojp.usdoj.gov/index.cfm?ty=pbdetail&iid=2316

According to the document cited, in 2009 there were 3,911,300 men under "community supervision either on probation or parole" and 2,086,400 men "held in the custody of state or federal prisons or local jails." The total of both groups was 5,997,700 men. There were about 1,241,625 men on active duty in the armed forces during the same year.

sources departments to protect their interests and their bottom lines. There is no "us." A legal entity can't care if you live or die, or if you're happy.

If you're a good boy, if you're well groomed and have a J-O-B and you learn to say the right things, maybe you can convince a nice girl to let you give her a baby and help her pay for it. If that's not your thing, you can spend your money getting drunk or busy yourself trying to hump whatever piece of ass strikes your fancy. Sex, after all, is social in the bonobo masturbation society. You'll have the hard won "right" to rub yourself against whatever makes you feel good, as long as you follow the rules.

If you're a good boy, you can curl up in the womb of your safe little Soviet-nouveau bloc apartment with your comfy stuff and enjoy your measured indulgences, your gourmet food, your micro-brew. You can busy yourself trying to master the art of erasing your own carbon footprint, or you can do your part by biking to work, weaving recklessly through a barrage of trucks and cars that could crush you for the sheer thrill of it. Maybe you'll take a class and get your permit and after another clerk confirms that you are competent enough to be licensed and properly insured, you'll be able to do something really crazy like ride a motorcycle. Maybe you'll pay someone to let you play a game or run a race or put on a safety harness and climb fake rocks. If not, you can always watch someone else do it on TV. Maybe you'll get yourself worked up about some petty inequity or injustice and participate in some non-violent resistance. Maybe you'll convince yourself that you are making a difference by standing in the same place with other people and shouting angrily at people who don't care. If you prefer, you can get online and vent your confused, impotent, vainglorious rage by playing the anonymous tough guy on some blog or forum. Or you can just say "fuck it" and spend all of your money on video games that give you the vicarious thrill of slaughtering hordes of aggressive "others." You can obsess over your fantasy football team. And there are always hobbies. You can find yourself something harmless and inoffensive to pass the time. Perhaps gardening. You can start a band or tinker with cars. Become a movie buff. You can paint little figurines of warriors. You can even get dressed up in costumes and do live-action role playing.

Whatever you do, just find some way to busy yourself.

There's nothing wrong with any of these things. All of them are "fun." What is "fun," if not masturbating your primal brain a little? I like having "fun." There's no harm in a little "fun" which is why it is called "fun"—and not something deadly serious, like "survival" or "war."

If that is all, if your life is all about chasing "fun," is that enough?

Is this level of civilization—is all of this peace and plenty—worth the cost?

How long will men be satisfied to replay and reinvent the conflict dramas of the past through books and movies and games, without the hope of experiencing any meaningful conflict in their own lives? When will we grow tired of hearing the stories of great men long dead?

How long will men tolerate this state of relative dishonor, knowing that their ancestors were stronger men, harder men, more courageous men—and knowing that this heritage of strength survives in them, but that their own potential for manly virtue, for glory, for honor, will be wasted?

We know what The Way of Men has been.

Is the way of the bonobo the only way that is left?

Day after day, day after day,
We stuck, nor breath nor motion;
As idle as a painted ship
Upon a painted ocean.

—Samuel Taylor Coleridge

"Rime of the Ancient Mariner"

WHAT IS BEST IN LIFE?

The Epic of Gilgamesh is one of the earliest known works of literature, and it is the product of one of the earliest complex civilizations. It tells the story of Gilgamesh, a mortal man of tremendous natural strength and prowess. No man could stand against Gilgamesh until a goddess fashioned an equal for him named Enkidu—a wild hairy man of warlike virtue who "knew nothing of the cultivated land."

Enkidu was friends will the animals and ranged the countryside helping them, causing woe for trappers and shepherds in the area. The men conspired against him. They sent a naked harlot to tempt Enkidu and tell him of Gilgamesh, and of wonders found in the luxurious city of Uruk, so that Enkidu would leave the hills and stop threatening their livelihood. Enkidu was curious, and he longed for a friend who was his peer, another man who would understand him. He followed the harlot to the tents of the shepherds, and she clothed Enkidu and introduced him to bread and strong wine. He joined the shepherds and hunted wolves and lions for them. With Enkidu as their watchman, they prospered.

A man came to Enkidu and reminded him of Gilgamesh and the city of Uruk, where Gilgamesh was behaving like a tyrant. Enkidu decided to go to the city and challenge Gilgamesh. The two men fought each other, snorting and shattering doorposts and shaking the walls like two bulls. As they grappled, they gained respect for each other and the two men decided to become friends.

Enkidu and Gilgamesh lived together in the city as brothers, but Gilgamesh was tormented by his own great potential and longed to do something that would be remembered. Enil, father of the gods, had given Gilgamesh "the power to bind and to loose, to be the darkness and the light of mankind." Enkidu complained to Gilgamesh that his own arms had grown weak, and that he was "oppressed by idleness." To fulfill their destinies, they knew they had to leave the comfort of the city and suffer and fight evil together. Gilgamesh cried out to the god Shamash:

> "Here in the city man dies oppressed at heart, man perishes with despair in his heart. I have looked over the wall and I see the bodies floating on the river, and that will be my lot also. Indeed I know it is so, for whoever is tallest among men cannot reach the heavens, and the greatest cannot encompass the earth. Therefore I would enter that country: because I have not established my name stamped on brick as my destiny decreed, I will go to the country where the cedar is cut. I will set up my name where the names of famous men are written; and where no man's name is written I will raise a monument to the gods.' The tears ran down his face and he said, 'Alas, it is a long journey that I must take to the Land of Humbaba. If this enterprise is not to be accomplished, why did you move me, Shamash, with the restless desire to perform it?"[1]

---

1   *The Epic of Gilgamesh*. Trans. N. K. Sanders. Penguin Classics, ePenguin, 1973. 61-72. Print. Loc 944-1091. Kindle.

If there is a "crisis of masculinity," this is it, and the problem is as old as civilization itself.

The true "crisis of masculinity" is the ongoing and ever-changing struggle to find an acceptable compromise between the primal gang masculinity that men have been selected for over the course of human evolutionary history, and the level of restraint required of men to maintain a desirable level of order in a given civilization.

Civilized life and technology offer many benefits to men. The simple, hardscrabble lives of our primitive ancestors may not have been as nasty, brutish or short as Hobbes believed, but it would be foolish to say that men have gained nothing from agricultural innovation or the division of labor. Without such changes there would have been no great works of art or literature, no great buildings or monuments, no printing press, no laptop for me to type on. Countless people have died throughout history from infections that anyone can cure today with cheap over-the-counter medications. We enjoy abundant foods and strong, imported wines and—perhaps most importantly—we have a steady supply of clean, drinkable water. Men wanted these things thousands of years ago when the Epic of Gilgamesh story was conceived.

Enkidu complained that he had grown weak and that he felt oppressed by the idleness of civilized life.

Men have known since Gilgamesh that civilization comes at a cost.

The manly virtues are raw and perishable. Males are on average naturally stronger, have a greater tendency to take risks, and they have a greater drive to master the world around them through technics—but all of these aptitudes require cultivation.

Muscles atrophy when improperly nourished and infrequently used. A man who never pushes his strength threshold will never even glimpse his physical potential, as anyone who has achieved substantial strength gains through physical training can attest. Strength is a "use it or lose it" aptitude.

Men may be natural risk-takers, but the increased confidence and surefootedness that we recognize as manly courage is the product of constant testing. The chest-thumping of untested men is hardly courage; Hobbes called it "vaine-glory", because "a well grounded confidence begetteth attempt; whereas the supposing of power does not."[2] Or, to put it in the words of Tyler Durden, "How much can you know about yourself, [if] you've never been in a fight?" Modern men are not merely lacking initiation into manhood, as some have suggested, they are lacking meaningful trials of strength and courage. Few modern men will truly "know themselves," as men, in the way that their forefathers did.

Likewise, skills must be mastered and practiced to be truly useful. Talent will only get you so far. If you are never truly challenged in a meaningful way and are only required to perform idiot-proofed corporate processes to get your meat and shelter, can you ever truly be engaged enough to call yourself alive, let alone a man?

Later in the Epic of Gilgamesh, after Gilgamesh killed the Bull of Heaven and overthrew the monstrous Humbaba, his comrade Enkidu died. Gilgamesh was distraught, and he searched for a way to cheat his own death. He met a young girl who made wine, and she told him that there was no way for him to avoid death. She told him to fill his belly with good things, to dance and be merry, to feast and rejoice. She told him to cherish his children and make his wife happy, "for this too is the lot of man."[3]

---

2   Hobbes, Thomas. *Leviathan*. 1651. Cambridge University Press, 1996. 42. Print.

3   *The Epic of Gilgamesh*. Trans. N. K. Sanders. Penguin Classics, ePenguin, 1973. 102. Print. Loc 1483. Kindle.

This *too*, is the lot of man.

In times of peace and plenty, when their bellies are full and they feel safe, women have always advised men to abandon manly pursuits and the way of the gang, to enjoy the safe pleasures of vicariousness and to join women in domestic life. When no threat is imminent, it has always been in the best interest of women to calm men down and enlist their help at home, raising children, and fixing up the grass hut. This is The Way of Women.

Men are people, too. It is not my intention to characterize men as soulless monsters who care about nothing but blood and glory. Men do love; sometimes more passionately and more unconditionally than women. Men can be tender and nurturing; any man who disputes that hates his father. Men write and tell stories and create things of remarkable beauty. All of these things can be part of being a man.

Men and women share much in common, but this book is not about the things that make men human, it is about the things that make them men.

Feminists dismiss biology and "outdated" ideas about masculinity and argue that men can change if they want to. Men do have free wills, and they *can* change to some extent, but men are not merely imperfect women. Men are individuals with their own interests, and they don't need women to show them how to be men. Women are not selfless spirit guides who have no interests or motivations of their own. Men have always had their own way, The Way of The Gang, and they've always inhabited a world apart from women.

"*Can* men change?" is the wrong question.

Better questions are: "Why *should* men change?" and "What does the average guy get out of the deal?"

When pressed to answer this question, feminists and men's rights activists never seem to be able to come up with anything but promises of increased financial and physical security and the freedom to show weakness and fear. Masses of men never rushed to the streets demanding the freedom to show weakness and fear, and they never braved gunfire or battle axes for the right to cry in public. Countless men, however, have died for the ideas of freedom and self-determination, for the survival and honor of their own tribes, for the right to form their own gangs.

Feminists, elite bureaucrats, and wealthy men all have something to gain for themselves by pitching widespread male passivity. The way of the gang disrupts stable systems, threatens the business interests (and social status) of the wealthy, and creates danger and uncertainty for women. If men can't figure out what kind of future they want, there are plenty of people who are ready to determine what kind of future they'll get.

They'll get a decorated cage.

They'll get a Fleshlight®, a laptop, a gaming console, a cubicle and a prescription drip.

They'll get some exciting new gadgets.

They'll get something that *feels* a little bit like being a man.

Women will continue to mock them, and they'll deserve it.

Lionel Tiger wrote that men "don't get what they're about not to have."[4] The world is changing, and men are being told that newer is always better, that change is inevitable, that the future feminists and globalists want is unavoidable. Men are

---

4   Tiger, Lionel. *The Decline of Males.* 1999. Golden Books. Print. 257.

being told that their future is logical, that it is moral, that it is better and that men had better learn to like it. But who is this new world really better *for?*

Civilization comes at a cost of manliness. It comes at a cost of wildness, of risk, of strife. It comes at a cost of strength, of courage, of mastery. It comes at a cost of honor. Increased civilization exacts a toll of virility, forcing manliness into further redoubts of vicariousness and abstraction. Civilization requires men to abandon their tribal gangs and submit to the will of one big institutionalized gang. Globalist civilization requires the abandonment of the gang narrative, of *us* against *them.* It requires the abandonment of human scale identity groups for "one world tribe." The same kind of men who once saw their own worth in the eyes of the peers who they depended on for survival will have to be satisfied with a "social security number" and the cheerfully manipulative assurances of their fellow drones. Feminist civilization requires the abandonment of patriarchy and brotherhood as men have known it since the beginning of time. The future being dreamed for us doesn't require the reimaging of masculinity; it ultimately demands the end of manhood and the soft embrace of personhood that has long been the feminist prescription for this ancient crisis of masculinity.

This end of men, this decline of males, this new bonobo masturbation society of peace and plenty—this No Man's Land—is not inevitable. It will require the tacit or expressed consent of billions of men. Like every civilization, it must be built on the backs of men, and most of them must agree to abide by and enforce its laws. You can't have prisons without prison guards and you can't have security without some kind of police. Men will have to get up in the morning and go to their clerking jobs and smile and consume and continue to amuse themselves according to regulation. Civilization requires a social contract, and men have to keep up their end of the bargain for it to work.

This future can only happen if men help create it.

As I wrote in the opening chapter of this book, men must choose a way.

To make this choice, they must ask themselves:

What is best in life?"

The "crisis of masculinity" poses exactly that philosophical question.

If you decide that true happiness for men lies in the elimination of risk, the satiation of hunger, the escape of labor and the pursuit of "fun," then our bonobo future may sound like some kind of One World Las Vegas.

I have come to the conclusion that the lot of man is to find a balance between the domestic world of comfort and the world of manly strife. Men cannot be men—much less good or heroic men—unless their actions have meaningful consequences to people they truly care about. Strength requires an opposing force, courage requires risk, mastery requires hard work, honor requires accountability to other men. Without these things, we are little more than boys playing at being men, and there is no weekend retreat or mantra or half-assed rite of passage that can change that. A rite of passage must reflect a real change in status and responsibility for it to be anything more than theater. No reimagined manhood of convenience can hold its head high so long as the earth remains the tomb of our ancestors. Men must have some work to do that's worth doing, some sense of meaningful action. It is not enough to be busy. It is not enough to be fed and clothed given shelter and safety in exchange for self-determination. Men are not ants or bees or hamsters. You can't just set up a plastic habitat and call it good enough. Men need to feel connected to a group of men, to have a sense of their place in it. They need a sense of identity that can't be bought at the mall. They need *us* and to have *us,* you must also have *them.* We are not wired for "one world tribe."

I've been a non-believer all of my life, but I'd drop to my knees and sing the praises of any righteous god who collapsed this Tower of Babel and scattered men across the Earth in a million virile, competing cultures, tribes, and gangs.

Honor as I understand the definition requires that kind of "diversity."

I don't say this because I think I'd personally fare better in a more primitive society. I spent the last six months reading and writing, not training for the zombie apocalypse.

I hope that men, to quote Guy Garcia, "yank at their chains and pull the entire temple down with them,"[5] because I hate to think that this is the end of The Way of Men. Everyone from schoolteachers to the United Nations is rushing to do away with "outmoded" models of masculinity, but they're not replacing it with anything better. In a review of Steven Pinker's book about violence, James Q. Wilson mentioned that the real change occurs when men care more about getting rich than getting bloody.[6] It's tragic to think that heroic man's great destiny is to become economic man, that men will be reduced to craven creatures who crawl across the globe competing for money, who spend their nights dreaming up new ways to swindle each other. That's the path we're on now.

What a withering, ignoble end…

---

5   Garcia, Guy (2008-10-07). *The Decline of Men* (p. 268). HarperCollins e-books. Kindle Edition.

6   Wilson, James Q. "Burying the Hatchet." *The Wall Street Journal* 1 Oct. 2011. Web. 4 Oct. 2011. http://online.wsj.com/article/SB100014240531119 04332804576537813826824914.html

Humanity needs to go into a Dark Age for a few hundred years and think about what it's done.

I prefer to not to use the words, 'let's stop something'.

I prefer to say, 'let's start something, let's start the world'.

—Peter Fonda, 2011

START THE WORLD

There is no democratic spur from our current path that can lead us back to The Way of Men.

The Men's Rights Movement seeks equity with women, and therefore points in the same direction as feminism. It wants to relieve men of making sacrifices on the behalf of women. It wants men and women alike to pursue individual prosperity without special, gendered obligations or clearly defined sex roles. The anger that drives the Men's Rights Movement comes from a sense that women aren't playing fairly, that they are cheating, that when given the chance they will use the rhetoric of equality to skew things in their own favor. The men are right about that. Women are re-designing the world in their own image. It is naïve for men to expect otherwise.

The Way of Men is to fight the external threat, and to fight other men. Sometimes men fight *over* women, but men have no history of fighting women. During times of peace and plenty it has always been the Way of Women to lure men to away from the volatile gang, to seek his investment in her re-productive endeavor, and to encourage him to seek refuge and comfort in domesticity. A comfortable man is less likely to take risks, and warriors have always known that too much comfort makes men soft. Men are not going to rise up and form one great political action committee to fight the influence of women. Men of means see too much immediate social and financial gain in catering to the interests of women. Politicians see a more politically and socially active population that must be appeased, and they will continue to fall all over themselves to get the female vote. Women are better suited to and better served by the globalism and consumerism of modern democracies that promise security, no-strings attached sex and shopping. For the most part, male bureaucrats cannot be counted on to help men who they don't know, when there is a political risk involved. Again, it is naïve for men to expect otherwise.

Another bulwark to social change on behalf of men is the reality of globalism. In America we are conditioned to think of corporations as "The Man," but that's a very Twentieth Century sense of things. Today's robber-barons and fat cats are figureheads that captain global enterprises which can basically function without them. The reigning presidents and CEOs are often as disposable as the workers. They come and go. There is no "Man." There is only the profit-driven, hydra-headed legal entity, whose workers make cost/benefit analyses to increase profit and further their own status and salary, usually with an eye on producing immediate, short-term results. Those workers don't care about what happens to a company in ten years, because if they are saavy and career-minded, they may well be working for a competitor by then. There is no "conspiracy" here, only people looking out for their immediate interests. If the legal department fears legal action, it will go through human resources and pre-empt it by initiating anti-sexist or anti-racist policies, or even soft affirmative action and public relations programs that reach out to litigious communities.

It is in the interest of corporate enterprises in most cases to champion anti-sexist (pro-feminist) and anti-racist policies because identity conflicts can be costly and inefficient. To the global corporation, people are interchangeable units of labor priced at different values. Your sexual or tribal identity is a

nuisance and a source of potential liability. Only thin identities are advantageous—like the kind of music or movies
you prefer. Thin identities are marketing niches. *Us* vs. *them*
identities and different sex roles are problematic and cumber-
some. But don't take my word for it, I'm a right-wing sex-
ist. America's favorite left-wing anarchist, Noam Chomsky,
wrote that "Capitalism basically wants people to be interchangeable cogs" and that differences among them are "usually not functional."[1] Chomsky was talking about race, but his
comments that corporations see people only as "consumers
and producers" and that "any other properties they might
have are kind of irrelevant, and usually a nuisance" can logi-
cally be applied to differences between men and women. The
genderless feminist utopia of humans who are neither masculine nor feminine is more efficient from the utilitarian per-
spective of the global enterprise. Don't expect the billions of
dollars that international corporations wield to move in favor
of men any time soon.

All of this is not to say that Men's Rights activists are
wrong or useless, but that they can only perform triage and
provide first aid. Men's Rights advocates can do things to
make the situation better for men in the short term, like work
for fairness in divorce proceedings and child custody cases
and sexual harassment lawsuits. They can call attention to the
lies and distortions of feminists, and they can work to dis-
credit feminist "experts" on masculinity who repackage the
same old 1970s boilerplate propaganda as "science" year after
year. This is good work. Like what passes for conservatism
today, it puts on a break that slows the degeneracy that feminists call "progress."

Women, individually, are not to blame for everything that
has transpired over the past few hundred years. Individual
women can certainly not be blamed for The Industrial Revo-

---

1   Chomsky, Noam. *Understanding Power: The Indispensable Chomsky.*
The New York Press, 2002. 88-89. Print.

lution. They can't be blamed for the trains, planes, and auto-
mobiles that make globalism possible. They can't be blamed
for Marxism, or the birth control pill, or the Internet or the
shopping mall. Women, as a group, can probably be blamed
for abominations like reality television, and for a lot of bad
music and art, and for making mainstream magazines almost
unreadably gossipy and stupid. But individual women, a
few figureheads aside, can't fairly be blamed for a whole lot.
Women are just acting according to their natures and skew-
ing things in their interests, as they've always wanted to, and
as men have prevented them from doing for most of human
history. It's not as though men have been selfless creatures,
historically speaking. Men and women alike can be tremen-
dously generous and self-sacrificing, but on an average day
we'll take care of our own interests first. That's the Way of
People.

The point of this book is not to portray women as evil
shrews. Women are humans who are slightly different from
men, and given the opportunity they will serve their own
slightly different interests and follow their own slightly different way. Women aren't evil, but they aren't angels, either.
They are what they are. No matter how much sympathy some
may have for the plight of modern men, women are not going
to give up what they have so long as they believe it's worth
having. They aren't going to rush to the polls to relieve themselves of advantages or support systems. As long as states
offer women peace and plenty, women and big government
will continue to enjoy a symbiotic relationship. Women can
be sympathetic, but they're not dumb.

Any return to The Way of Men will fail to receive bipar-
tisan support.

I also doubt that men will ever assert their interests as a
sex through violent revolution. It's not realistic. There's no
good pitch for it. Men aren't going to make the streets run
red with their own blood for...well...what exactly would

they even ask for? Men aren't going to rise up and storm the Capitol to demand the repeal of the Nineteenth Amendment. It would be easier to get them to riot in Washington D.C. to repeal the Sixteenth Amendment and end Federal Income Tax—something women could get on board with, too—and that isn't happening anytime soon. The closest thing they've managed in recent years was the Tea Party movement which, despite early media hysteria that it was a mob of angry white men, was quickly co-opted by women like Sarah Palin and Michelle Bachmann, who ended up turning it into something more like a tent revival potluck for heavily armed soccer moms.

Even if men were inclined to organize against the State in its current form, men would lose before they even started. The state has the ability to seek out and identify anti-state movements who plan to use violence, and has crushed organized armed resistance movements on numerous occasions. Men aren't dumb, either. Organized, armed resistance movements end in "death by cop" long before they gain the money, the numbers, or the momentum necessary to make themselves a viable threat. This ain't Africa or Central America.

But what if it were?

What if the United States *were* a little bit more like Mexico?

I worked with an illegal immigrant for a while, and he told me that while he loved his homeland and his culture, he didn't want to raise his family in a place without law and order. He told me stories about police shaking down drivers for cash instead of writing tickets. When I visited a border town a few years ago, it was striking how blurry the line was between the *Federales* and a gang. There was no "officer friendly." The *Federales* were a bunch of guys with assault rifles whose purpose was clearly to observe and intimidate. When they got a call, they jumped on the back of what looked like a Ford F150 with an aftermarket roll bar and made off in a cloud of desert dust. In other places, the *Federales* don't look so tough. It's not unusual for Mexican police to wear ski masks at work, for fear of gang retribution.[2]

That retribution can be brutal, as it was recently in the border town of Guadalupe, where a female police chief went missing around Christmas in 2010.

> "Erika Gandara was a former radio dispatcher for the police department in the town of 9,000, which is just across the U.S. border, one mile from Fabens, Texas. The previous police chief was murdered and decapitated; his head was found in an ice chest. Gandara, 28, a single woman with no children, was the only applicant for the job and its salary of $580 per month.
>
> One policeman was murdered during Gandara's first week on the job. By the time she became chief, the entire force of eight patrolmen had either been killed or fled. She was the sole law enforcement representative in a Juarez valley town that was part of the war between competing drug cartels for access routes into the U.S."[3]

---

2   "Drug violence mars Mexico city." *BBC News*. Ed. Stephanie Gibbs. BBC News, Cancun, 19 Feb. 2009. Web. 4 Oct. 2011. http://news.bbc.co.uk/2/hi/americas/7897345.stm

3   Harrigan, Steve. "America's Third War: As Drug Cartels Continue Stronghold, Female Mexican Police Chief Taken Near Christmas Still Missing." *FoxNews.com*. Ed. Steve Harrigan. 8 Feb. 2011. Web. 4 Oct. 2011. http://www.foxnews.com/us/2011/02/08/americas-war-female-mexican-chief-police-missing-christmas

In September 2011, *Reuters* reported that violence was slowing down in Tijuana after years of bloodshed, in part because the gangs there had finally settled a turf war and one gang established near-complete control over the area. [4]

If men are going to re-assert their interests and return to The Way of Men, they're not going to do it through a democratic movement or a social movement or an armed political uprising. They're going to do it in a way that looks a lot more like what *La Familia* was doing with John Eldredge's work. They're going to do it through gangs, in areas of the world where the State has lost power and credibility. They're going to take some of the ideas from surviving male traditions and repurpose them to create their own unique identities, their own *us*.

The current level of security we enjoy (or fear, depending on what side of the law you're on) is very, very expensive, and the United States is a very large territory. The quality of policing we have today is the direct result of our wealth and status as a major world power. Our police are on a payroll, and less money will mean fewer police, more frustrated police, and more police corruption. As the power of the State wanes, non-state actors gain breathing room and influence. The United States is far bigger than North Korea, and the United States is not China. Mao had to kill over forty million people to get the Chinese on the same page. Not including those who died in various famines, it seems to have taken Stalin at least three million deaths to keep the Soviets in order. His tyranny gave birth to the *Vory v Zakone,* or "Thieves in Law," who represent only a small portion of the crime syndicates currently active in

---

4   "Tijuana violence slows as one cartel takes control." *http://www.reuters.com*. Ed. Lizbeth Diaz. Reuters, 5 Sept. 2011. Web. 4 Oct. 2011. http://www.reuters.com/article/2011/09/05/us-mexico-drugs-tijuana-idUS-TRE7844EX20110905

modern Russia.5 Criminal gangs are active all over the United States, especially in border zones and ghettos where policing is inadequate or viewed as illegitimate and tyrannical, as it by many blacks who see the police as inherently racist, and in areas with high concentrations of illegal immigrants who see themselves as unfairly persecuted. For many, the State is already the "other."

In the film *Gran Torino*, Clint Eastwood's character Walt Kowalski confessed to Father Janovich that one of his "sins" was failing to pay taxes on a private sale he had made several years prior. He said, "It's the same as stealing." That's the country my grandfather lived in. Many people who grew up before the Vietnam era felt *that* connected to their nation. They were invested in it. The United States was *us*, or truer to the spirit of it, it was "we the people."

In the post-Vietnam era, it seems as though more and more people on the Left and the Right alike regard the government as "them." Whether they consider themselves Democrats, Republicans, or Independents of some kind, whether they make twenty thousand dollars a year or two hundred thousand dollars a year, most people today will pour over their tax returns looking for any way they can find to pay *less*. Few would give a second thought to claiming profits on a sale they've made using a craigslist ad. If you told them it was their civic duty, they'd probably give you the look they save for Jehovah's Witnesses. Small business owners usually find ways to cut corners, and many are happy to hide income or hire workers illegally or under the table to avoid paying taxes or dealing with complicated regulations. Every year average Americans download billions of dollars worth of pirated music and movies. Like smoking marijuana—the same pot that Mexican gangs are trafficking—these things have become socially acceptable practices at almost every level of society.

---

5   Schwirtz, Michael. "Vory v Zakone has hallowed place in Russian criminal lore." *New York Times*. N.p., 29 July 2008. Web. 4 Oct. 2011. http://www.nytimes.com/2008/07/29/world/europe/29iht-moscow.4.14865004.html

The Italians have a saying for this. *Tutti colpevoli, nessuno colpevole.*

It means, "If everyone is guilty, no one is guilty."

Walt Kowalski's America is long gone.

Globalism and nationalism have irreconcilable ends. Globalism is undermining our sense of national identity, our connection to the government. The American economy was placed in the hands of globalists—*all* recent administrations have promoted and said starry eyed things about the magic of the global economy—and now the economy is like a plate being balanced on a stick by a circus clown. There's a lot of funny money out there spinning around, and any number of factors could send us further into financial decline. We're dependent on cheap imported technology, cheap imported food, cheap imported fuel. A dramatic spike in gas prices or a major national disaster could easily turn a volatile place like Southern California into a war zone. States are selling their own toll highways to foreign nations for short term cash infusions. There's already a sense among people under forty that the money they pay into Social Security won't be there—or won't be worth anything—by the time they get old. People who work know they are throwing money into a black hole. Others are working the system and taking whatever they can get. Without endless economic growth, the United States won't be able to make good on its promises of endless prosperity and security. As things get worse and the State seems powerless to help, the State will seem less and less legitimate. People will lose their moral connection to it. Laws will seem more like revenue traps and shakedowns. The state will start to seem more like another extortion racket, and, as in Mexico, people will have a harder time telling the good guys from the bad guys. The U.S. of *us* will become the U.S. of *them* and we'll Balkanize from within. If not officially, then unofficially. It's already happening.

The new Way of Women depends on prosperity, security, and globalism.

Any return of honor and The Way of Men and the eventual restoration of balance and harmony between the sexes will require the weakening of all three.

One of my favorite books is Anthony Burgess' *The Wanting Seed*. It's a sci-fi novel that tells the story of a future when, due to overpopulation, the State encourages homosexuality and effeminacy and officially discourages reproductive families. Throughout the book, Burgess writes about a theory of cyclical history that moves through three phases: *Pelphase, Interphase*, and *Gusphase*. In the Gusphase, named after St. Augustine, humanity is viewed through the eyes of a stern father who expects men to be violent and untrustworthy. Men see only what Peterson and Wrangham would call the "demonic" in each other and those who seek order rule with an iron fist. After a period of security, people demonstrate that they can behave reasonably well, and men start to think that people are not so bad after all. Thinking shifts into the Pelphase mode, named for St. Pelagius, wherein men see each other as intrinsically good, peaceful, and perfectible through the gentle, guiding touch of social reform. However, this rose colored, "noble savage" view of man does not reflect his nature, either. Man can't always be trusted to always follow the rules. He plays the system and does what he wants, and that leads to distrust, disorder, and disillusionment. This is when, as Burgess put it:

"Disappointment opens up a vista of chaos."[6]

---

    6   Burgess, Anthony. *The Wanting Seed*. W.W. Norton & Co., 1962. 19. Print.

During the middle phase of the cycle, called Interphase, there is violence and chaos and tyranny. It's a great shake-up that brings about another Gusphase, and eventually, a new Pelphase, and the cycle continues.

Men will not reassert themselves in any meaningful way through additional tweaking of an optimistic Pelagian system that is based on a pleasant denial of human nature. Men will reassert their interests during the Interphase. When states weaken and become "hollow" as futurist John Robb[7] believes they will, men will assert their interests through a return to their most basic social form. When the aching womb of the state can no longer provide the services or the security that keep men passive and dependent, localized groups of men who trust each other will build smaller networks to protect and further their own interests. In the presence of weak tyranny and the absence of strong nationalism, the shepherds will gather round their Robin Hoods, and they will found new tribes.

In the chaos that follows disappointment, gangs of men can restart the world.

Their future—the one world nanny state from cradle to grave, the global civilization of managers and clerks, the thin consumer identities, the bonobo masturbation society—is already showing signs of stress. *Their future* is based on unsustainable illusions and lies about human nature. *Their future* requires too many men to deny their own immediate interests to serve an abstract "greater good" that is far beyond human scale. All over the world, the *Star Trek* future that was once considered "inevitable" is starting to look improbable. The European Union is struggling, the global economy is faltering, and every day more people are starting to acknowledge that America is in a decline from which it will not recover.

---

7   See Robb's http://globalguerrillas.typepad.com/globalguerrillas/ site for articles and up-to-the-minute thinking about "hollow states" and creating "resilient communities."

Their future is already falling. It just needs a push.

If you want to push things toward The Way of Men and start the Interphase, create disappointment.

Throughout 2011, "Occupy Wall Street" protesters camped out in public parks across the country. They were angry about something. They weren't sure what. Their messages were incoherent. They were desperate. They wanted the government to come to their rescue. They wanted the government to fix things. They wanted the government to stop "corporate greed" as if it is possible to demand that global corporations stop acting to maximize profit. The "occupants" still just barely believed the dream that the State is beholden to the will of the people. They still wanted to believe that the State cares what they want. They wanted to believe that the state wants them to be happy. They were emotionally attached to the idea that the government cares, but they already suspected that it doesn't.

It doesn't, because it can't. Like global corporations, States have escaped human scale. There is no "man" to fight. States are institutions whose ultimate goals are survival, perpetuation, and expansion.

When the protesters went home, they achieved nothing. Nothing changed, though a few talking heads offered reassurances that the protesters had been heard.

People need to stop looking to the State for help and direction. They must become disillusioned and disappointed. To push things in a direction that is ultimately—though not immediately—better for men, the emotional connection between the people and the state must be severed completely. When the body of the people is released from the head of the sovereign, chaos will ensue. In that chaos, men will find themselves. They will stop looking to the State for help, and start looking to each other. Together, men can create smaller, tighter, more localized systems

People say they want a world that's more rational, but a world that's out of step with human nature isn't more rational at all.

Men aren't getting more rational.

They're getting weaker.

They're getting more fearful.

They're giving up more and more control.

There is no high road.

The only way out for men is The Way of the Gang.

HOW TO START A GANG

Any return to The Way of Men is probably going to happen in hollow states through extra-legal means. Gangs form out of necessity, or to exploit opportunities. Gangs are going to gain the most traction in areas where State influence is weak, creating both necessity and opportunity. Furthermore, gangs are proto-states. Proto-states threaten the power of larger existing states, so when men form proto-states to assert their own interests, their actions will be outlawed by those states.

It is not my intent here to tell you how to start a criminal enterprise.

I have romanticized gangs somewhat to make a point about the nature of men, but I am not suffering from any delusion that modern gangs are run by "good guys" who take from the rich and give to the poor. I have every reason to believe that life in a gang today would be nasty, brutish, and short. I have every reason to believe that life in a gang existing inside a collapsed State would be nasty, brutish, and short. There is no shortage of evidence about gang brutality, infighting, human trafficking, rape, or murder almost for the sake of murder alone. Wrangham and Peterson called the gang impulse male "demonism" for some good reasons.

The conclusion I reached while writing this book was that the gang is the kernel of masculine identity. I believe it is also the kernel of ethnic, tribal, and national identity. The culture of the gang is, as author bell hooks wrote in a rather different context, "the essence of patriarchal masculinity."[1]

If you want to follow The Way of Men, if you want to advance a return to honor and manly virtue, if you want to steel yourself against an uncertain future—start a gang.

Honor requires an honor group, a group of men with similar values. Honor requires the possibility of dishonor in the eyes of peers whose respect you value. The cultivation of manly virtue is accelerated by completion and the expectations of male peers. And, if you want to become resilient to uncertainty and chaos, you need a circle of men who you trust and who you can depend on.

Some readers will inevitably respond: "My wife/girlfriend is awesome. She takes boxing and shoots guns and fixes cars. She's my partner."

That's nice. But if your strategy for the future is holing up with ma and the chillins, your strategy sucks. I don't care if your girlfriend is a Certified Ninja, she's not worth eight men. *Kill Bill* was not a documentary. A strong and skillful woman will be worth more to you in a crisis than a *prima donna*, but she can't replace men in your life. No woman can take the place of men in a man's life.

It is evolutionarily sound for women to want to secure your commitment to them and attempt to place themselves at the center of your world. They'll want to be involved in everything you do, and they'll be on guard against perceived threats to their security and your commitment.

---

1   hooks, bell (2007-03-16). *We Real Cool* (p. 26). Taylor & Francis. Kindle Edition.

Men have been negotiating the "crisis of masculinity"— the push and pull between civilized domesticity and lure of gang life—for centuries. Men need to set boundaries and make time for men in their lives. It's important to their sense of identity, it's important to their sense of security and belonging, and it's good survival strategy. Part of the reason we are where we are right now is that men stopped depending on each other and started depending on the State. The family unit is not enough. A support network of ten is better than a support network of two.

To get a sense of how one might go about expanding that support network and "start a gang," here's a working definition of what a gang really is, based on the idea of men bonding, creating a group identity and setting up a perimeter:

Gang - A bonded, hierarchical coalition of males allied to assert their interests against external forces.

A gang is essentially a male group identity, it's an *us*. It's a go-to group of men allied against *them*.

In an emergency situation, the *us* is often defined by proximity. You've seen the movie. A bunch of unlikely characters get stuck together by unforeseen circumstances and are forced to work out their differences and learn to depend on each other. That could certainly happen, but depending on the luck of the draw isn't a great strategy. Picking your team is a better strategy.

Create Proximity

The Internet is a good filter. It's a good way to find men who share some of your values. However, your friends on message boards and on social networking sites, scattered all over the world, are not going to be there for you when the proverbial shit hits the fan. Spend more time making contact with men who are geographically close to you. If you have close friends in your area, consider moving into the same apartment complex or within a few blocks of one another. Think about the way gangs start in inner cities. Men and boys have lived and died to defend tribes with territories as small as a few blocks. Proximity creates familiarity and shared identity. It creates *us*. Spreading our alliances across nations and continents keeps us reliant on the power of the State and the global economy. Men who are separated and have no one else to rely on must rely on the State.

Choose Your *Us*

A lot of factors could define the boundaries of *us* against *them*. If your religion is important to you, that's a good place to start. Mormon men, for instance, would probably fall into a community gang fairly easily. If your ethnic heritage or race is something you feel strongly about, as is very often the case with gangs, then that might be your starting point. Familiarity and likeness make trust easier to establish. However, sports teams make out well enough with men from very different backgrounds. If a desirable superordinate goal—like *survival*—is introduced, it has been proven that men can put aside all sorts of differences.

Men with opposing viewpoints can respect each other and enjoy civilized debates, but when it comes to forming *us*, it's better to have a group of men who are on the same page about the issues most important to them.

If you have decided after reading this book that you want to return to The Way of Men, the men in your gang will have to be committed to undermining the globalist masturbation society, hollowing out the State, and reviving a culture of honor.

Create Fraternity

A gang is a fraternity, a bonded brotherhood of men. That said; don't start trying to figure out your colors or your secret handshake just yet. These kinds of male cultural phenomena will occur organically as the result of shared history and identity. Only huge organizations like the Army can effectively sort a bunch of men into a group and artificially create a gang or brotherhood. It is possible for political movements to do this, but if they appear to be openly anti-government, their high profile is going to attract the attention of the authorities.

You don't need a formal group or a membership charter, and you don't need to elect a president. What you need is face time. You can bond with men online, but only to a point. People can hide online in ways that they can't in person. Men are tactical thinkers. They guard themselves. To get to know a man you need to spend time with him, you need to do things together, you need to build trust. Don't expect a casual acquaintance to have your back when you're in trouble. A solid friendship is just like any other relationship. It requires give and take. It requires some time and some history.

If you know some guys you can connect with, and who are on more or less the same page philosophically, make sure you make time for them. Set aside time to create that history and build that trust. Even women who are "like one of the guys" will have a chilling effect on that process. Men are not honest with each other in the same way when women are present, and establishing trust requires honesty. Men are going to want to have girlfriends and wives and families and other connections with women in their lives, and that is all well and good, but as I said, you can't expect men who don't really know you to help you through tough times. Put in the effort. Eating and drinking together is fine, but it makes more sense to plan tactically oriented outings. You need to learn how to read each other and work together as a group. Go to the shooting range. Go hunting. Play paintball. Go to the gym. Take martial arts classes. Join a sports team. Take a workshop. Learn a useful skill. Fix something. Build something. Make something. Get off your asses and *do* something.

In harder times, the men that you do these kinds of things with are going to be the first men you call. They will be your gang. They will be your *us*.

I'm going to close this book with some Viking wisdom concerning male friendship from *The Sayings of Hár*, also known as the *Hávamál*.

If friend thou hast   whom faithful thou deemest,

And wishest to win him for thee:

Open thy heart to him   nor withhold thy gifts,

And fare to find him often.

If faithful friend   thou hast found for thee,

Then fare thou find him full oft;

Overgrown is soon   with tall grass and bush

The trail which is trod by no one.[2]

2   *The Poetic Edda.* Trans. Lee M. Hollander. 2nd ed. University of
Texas Press, 1962. 21, 32. Print. (The archaic "Ope" in the Hollander was up-
dated in this text to "open" for clarity.)

ACKNOWLEDGEMENTS

Writing this book required substantial sacrifices of my time, money, and attention; I'd like to thank my guileless compadre Lucio for his loyalty and support. My Vulcan friend Trevor Blake and I have been trading ideas about manliness over drinks and cigars for years, and his pages of notes provided much food for thought. When I thought I had finished the book the first time, writer Scott Locklin convinced me to gut it and rework it. *The Way of Men* is far better for that. I'd also like to thank Troy Chambers, Greg Johnson, and Jef Costello for their helpful notes and suggestions. I offer my thanks to Brett McKay for replying to my interview request. Few men spend as much time thinking about "The Art of Manliness" as he does.

All of the men I know have influenced my thinking about manhood—my father, my grandfathers, my friends, even men I have only met briefly or interacted with on occasion. All men have something to say about being a good man, and about being good at being a man. I'd like to thank Jesse and Max, my good pals and high ranking members of my apocalypse fireteam, for their perspectives on "what is best in life" and the finer points of alpha psychology.

Many thanks also to Bill Price and Richard Spencer for their interest in my work, and for helping me to build a larger audience of men who contributed to my thoughts on masculinity through comments and suggestions.

I consulted many books and articles while writing *The Way of Men*. Only a handful of them are cited. The book *A World of Gangs* by John Hagedorn was particularly influential. *Manliness* by Harvey C. Mansfield is also an important book.

Ideas about manliness that I partially or completely disagree with are dealt with in a short book titled *No Man's Land*, which was released for online in late 2011. The arguments in that book were included in the first draft of *The Way of Men*, but were cut to make the text lighter, faster, and more clearly about one idea. If this book left you wondering how my thoughts on masculinity fit into the larger contemporary debate about the subject, I urge you to read *No Man's Land* as a supplement to *The Way of Men*. Currently, you can download it for free at my web site:

jack-donovan.com/axis/no-mans-land/

FOR ESSAYS, NEWS, AND REVIEWS

JACK-DONOVAN.COM

ALSO BY JACK DONOVAN

**2009   BLOOD-BROTHERHOOD
AND OTHER RITES OF MALE ALLIANCE**
CO-AUTHORED WITH NATHAN F. MILLER

2007   ANDROPHILIA
SCAPEGOAT PUBLISHING

ALSO FROM DISSONANT HUM

2012   ALL ABOUT WOMEN
BY SIMON SHEPPARD

DISSONANT HUM
2012

CPSIA information can be obtained at www.ICGtesting.com
Printed in the USA
BVOW03s0814180414

351049BV00002B/13/P